Kings and Queens

Elizabeth Gundrey

Kings and Queens

text illustrations by Juliet Stanwell-Smith
cover illustration by Jene Hawkins

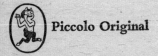

Piccolo Original

Pan Books

First published in Great Britain 1977
by Pan Books Ltd, Cavaye Place, London SW10 9PG
© Elizabeth Gundrey 1977
ISBN 0 330 25185 6
Printed in Great Britain by
Richard Clay (The Chaucer Press) Ltd
Bungay, Suffolk

Introduction

This book tells the story of the monarchs who have ruled England, Wales and (from the time of James I) Scotland. It's different from other books on this subject because every page represents ten years: so a monarch who ruled approximately ten years occupies one page, while one who ruled about thirty years gets three pages. This immediately gives you a good idea of the passing of time as one monarch succeeds another.

All rulers have had an effect on our country's history, even in recent years when Parliament has wielded more power than any king. Some have had a good influence and some not; some have made peace and others war; where one monarch may have done great things for the spread of law and justice, another may have left his mark on architecture, the church or the navy.

The story of the monarchy is full of variety and of drama, and when you travel about or go on holiday you are likely to spot many reminders of what each king or queen achieved. Pages 103–10 give you some ideas of things to look out for.

The Norman kings   1066–1154
The Plantagenets   1154–1485
The Tudors   1485–1603
The Stuarts   1603–1714
The Hanoverians   1714–1917
The Windsors   1917–

(George V changed the family name to Windsor when the German name, Hanover, was unpopular.)

William I 1066–1087

Age 39–60. Son of Duke Robert of Normandy.
Married Matilda (Flemish). Nine children. Died from injuries.
Buried at Caen (France).

To the Frenchman William, England was just a conquest to be added to his own far more important dukedom of Normandy. He wanted the country for its riches – to pay the armies needed for the struggles with other French rulers.

William had always been at war with one enemy or another. It had turned him into a tough, aggressive man. He was red-faced, tall and stout, and had never learned to read or to write.

William had first been plunged into a kill-or-be-killed life when he was only seven. His father, the Duke of Normandy, and his mother were unmarried (the boy was known contemptuously as William the Bastard) and when his father died in 1035 while on a pilgrimage to Jerusalem, others tried to seize the dukedom from young William, even sending assassins to kill his guardians. By the age of sixteen, William was himself leading his men into battle against such rebels, and so he learned early the skills of war.

Through his mother William was distantly related to Edward the Confessor, who then ruled over much of England. In 1051 the ageing Edward had promised him the English throne after his death, but later he changed his mind, and when he died in 1066 it was to Edward's brother-in-law Harold that the throne went.

William was furious. All through that summer he built wooden ships, gathered horses together, built wooden forts to be transported to England, and had huge stocks of chain-mail and weapons forged for his soldiers. But by the time he was ready to sail for England, there were gales blowing, and, fuming with impatience, he had to wait.

As it turned out, the delay was a piece of good luck, for in the meantime, England was being assailed by other invaders – the Vikings. King Harold's army marched north to York to drive them out, so it was exhausted and a week's march away by the time William was able to land in Sussex in September.

As William leapt ashore, he fell and clutched at the ground. 'An omen!' cried one of his knights. 'You already have a grip on the soil of England.' On 14 October the prophecy came true: William's victory at the battle of Hastings was total. For hours the English, armed with axes and spears, stood on a small hill withstanding repeated attacks by the Norman archers and mounted knights. But at sunset, imagining the Normans were in retreat, their ranks broke. Harold himself was killed by an arrow.

William and his men then marched through the countryside, destroying as they went, until they reached London, where on Christmas Day he was crowned in the newly built Westminster Abbey.

For years to come, local revolts continued against him (Hereward the Wake led the one at Ely), but he crushed each ruthlessly. All but a few landowners had their estates taken and given to Norman barons, who were required in return to keep William supplied with fighting men – the so-called 'feudal' system. The French language was spoken everywhere. Stone was brought from Normandy to build the formidable castles needed to keep the country subdued, Frenchmen were made bishops, and the English were forced to hand over money or goods.

William did bring some benefits, though. Law and order were maintained so that, as a writer of the time said, 'a man might go over his kingdom with his bosom full of gold ... and no man durst slay another.' He introduced the round-arched Norman style of architecture, massive and almost indestructible, so that to this day his castles, such as the Tower of London, and cathedrals, such as Durham, St Albans and Ely, can still be visited. He created the New Forest in Hampshire as a game reserve. 'He loved the tall red deer as if he were their father', it was said – but what he really loved was to hunt them.

In 1086 William decided to dispatch inspectors throughout the country to list details of all property – even every pig and every plough. The information was written down in two huge parchment volumes. Because all this recording seemed like the last day of judgment to the peasants, they called it the *Domesday Book* (doom's day). William planned to use this information to exact even more taxes; but he had to return to Normandy to deal with trouble there. In the course of a siege, William's horse stumbled and he died from the injuries.

William II 1087–1100

*Age about 27–40. Son of William I. Unmarried. Killed while hunting.
Buried in Winchester Cathedral.*

William the Conqueror bequeathed Normandy to his eldest son Robert
(even though he had rebelled against his father); but he left England to
his favourite, William. William, nicknamed Rufus because his face was
red like his father's, had to spend the first part of his reign putting down
revolts inspired by Robert; or else building defences, such as Carlisle
Castle, along the borders.

In 1096 William went to Normandy, which his good-for-nothing
brother Robert was by now glad to hand over to him for a large loan
(with which he departed on one of the Crusades). Now revolts in
Normandy too had to be suppressed and, as always, William Rufus was
as successful as he was tough. 'In war he enjoyed such success you would
think the whole world smiling upon him,' said a writer of the time.

But his world ceased smiling one summer evening when, while hunting
in the New Forest, he was killed by an arrow and his body was brought,
dripping with blood, on a farm wagon to Winchester for burial. An
accident? Or was it – murder?

One man in particular stood to gain by William's death. This was his
younger brother Henry who was also hunting in the forest at the time,
and who galloped instantly to Winchester
to take possession of the royal treasure
which was kept there, and then on
to London to be crowned king.
For him the death of his brother
occurred in the nick of time, since Robert
(still eager to possess England) was
soon due back from the Crusades.
Henry had motive and opportunity,
but we will never know whether
he played any part in his
brother's death.

Henry I 1100—1135

Age 32–67. Son of William I. Married Edith (Scottish) then Adela (French).
Two children. Died from food-poisoning.
Buried in Reading Abbey, Berkshire.

Henry was the first king of England to be able to read (he was nicknamed Beauclerk) and he enjoyed the company of learned men more than that of warriors. He also liked money, animals (he started a zoo) and peace. During his long reign there was no war in England.

As soon as he was crowned, he issued a charter proclaiming that he would put an end to the unjust practices of William II and rule the English fairly. He invited back Archbishop Anselm whom William had exiled; he married a Scottish princess in order to ensure that Scotland would stop its attacks on England; and, in the expectation that his brother Robert would try to invade England, which he did unsuccessfully in 1101, Henry made treaties with France and Flanders (now Belgium) to keep his brother in check.

Henry realized, however, that more than this would be needed to keep the peace in England. The barons who had plotted with Robert in the past were sure to do so again unless their power was broken. Their ringleader was the Earl of Shrewsbury, so Henry captured his strongholds and banished him to France. This was not the end of the matter, however, and the Earl continued to make trouble from Normandy, so that at last Henry sailed to meet him in battle there. The King returned victorious with not only the Earl as prisoner but his own brother Duke Robert too. Robert spent the rest of his life in captivity in Cardiff while Henry took control of Normandy.

Meantime, even though Henry's attitude to the Church was more understanding than William II's had been, there was conflict brewing. The clergy were no longer willing to have their abbots and bishops receive their staffs of office from a king. Archbishop Anselm felt so strongly about this that, once again, he chose to leave England. Only when the Pope threatened to excommunicate Henry did he give in and agree that these ceremonies should be performed by the Archbishop. More than mere ceremonial was involved; in yielding this point Henry was admitting that kings were not holy or divinely appointed.

Nevertheless, the common people continued to believe this for centuries to come, and in fact it was in Henry's reign that 'touching for the king's evil' first started. 'King's evil' was another name for the skin disease scrofula, and the superstitious believed that if the king touched someone suffering from this disease, he would be healed.

Like the kings before him, Henry had to spend a lot of time in Normandy defending it from its enemies, and the English were taxed heavily to pay for his armies. In 1119 he tried to put an end to wars with the neighbouring country of Anjou by marrying his only son, aged sixteen, to the old Count of Anjou's daughter. But within a year his son was drowned when the royal vessel, the *White Ship*, foundered on a rock in the Channel.

His only surviving child now was Maud, the twenty-two-year-old widow of the Emperor of Germany. So Henry attempted to make an alliance by marrying her against her will to the Count of Anjou. The Norman barons did not like the idea of Anjou, their recent enemy, becoming their ruler after Henry's death, and so conflict within Normandy started up once more. Before he could do much about this, Henry fell ill from 'a surfeit of lampreys' (overeating eels), and died.

Henry had been a successful king, keeping the peace, building up stores of wealth, and protecting the English peasants from exploitation by their Norman overlords. But he was ruthless and cruel. His father had never used the death penalty for crimes; Henry would have as many as forty-four thieves hanged in just one day. He caused men who forged coins to have their hands cut off, and he himself once threw a rebel off the battlements of a castle. He kept his own brother in prison for twenty-eight years.

Nevertheless, he set up a King's Court where the law was clearly seen to be upheld by judges who were not under the control of powerful barons. For this he earned the title Lion of Justice. He started a system of law enforcement from which we still benefit today; and along with this he created the Exchequer, an efficient department for collecting taxes, still a very necessary part of today's government.

Stephen 1135–1154

Age about 38–57. Nephew of Henry I. Married Matilda (French).
Three children. Buried in Faversham Abbey (Kent).

After Henry's death England was plunged into conflict. The barons refused to be governed by a woman, and offered the throne to Henry's favourite nephew Stephen instead of to his daughter Maud.

Stephen was a charming but weak man, Maud a haughty and powerful woman who had no intention of letting her rightful heritage go. She and her husband (Count Geoffrey of Anjou) gathered an army together and invaded England in 1139. Some of the barons decided to support her, others sided with Stephen, and meantime the Welsh and Scots seized the opportunity to cross their borders and pillage the English countryside.

In 1139 Stephen actually took Maud prisoner but, with more gallantry than wisdom, let her go. She then set herself up as Queen in Devizes (Wiltshire), holding court and issuing charters while Stephen ruled in London. Two years later, Stephen himself was taken prisoner in a battle and Maud went to London to be crowned. Her high-handed ways offended the Londoners, however, and they drove her out. Stephen's devoted wife rallied his armies and soon he was released to go in pursuit of Maud and her men again, besieging them in a castle at Oxford where they had taken refuge. She escaped by a rope hung from the castle walls and, camouflaged in a white cloak because there was snow on the ground, crossed the frozen river and passed unnoticed between the King's sentries.

In 1148 Maud gave up trying to gain the throne and left for Normandy, where she and her husband did succeed in wresting control from Stephen, who never again went back to Normandy to assert his rights there.

In the year before Stephen's death, hostilities were truly ended at last when, his son and heir having just died, the King agreed to adopt Maud's son, Henry (who had already made two invasion attempts) as his successor instead. Thus the line of Norman kings came to an end.

A brave, warm-hearted man, Stephen had behaved better towards the clergy than other Norman kings. He founded two huge abbeys,

Barrow-in-Furness and Faversham where he and his wife are buried, and gave many new liberties to the Church (perhaps to make up to the bishops whom he had earlier imprisoned when he suspected them of siding with Maud). But for six years of his reign the country had been burned and wrecked, churches were converted into forts, and local feuds flared up unchecked. Personal bravery and piety were not enough to make Stephen into an effective ruler in a century when the barons were always on the lookout for opportunities to stir up trouble and seize more power for themselves.

Henry II 1154–1189

Age 21–56. Grandson of Henry I. Married Eleanor (French).
Eight children. Buried at Fontevrault (France).

Henry II started a new royal family in England, the Plantagenets, who set a different style from the Norman warrior kings. Their name came from *planta genista*, the Latin for yellow broom flower, which the Counts of Anjou wore as an emblem on their helmets. The first Plantagenet kings were the Angevins, from Anjou, and later followed the related families of Lancaster and of York – fourteen monarchs all told, their reigns stretching over three centuries.

The youthful Henry was destined to be one of Europe's greatest kings, inheriting lands that reached from the north of England right to the Mediterranean coast. The centre of his empire was of course Anjou not England where he in fact spent only thirteen years of his long reign. But more than that vast princedom made him great.

Henry had been very well educated and loved reading. A broad man, plainly dressed and with close-cropped hair, freckled and bandy-legged from continual riding, Henry enjoyed difficulty and danger and had the boundless energy to travel ceaselessly and at top speed over his vast empire, bringing order wherever he went. But when he came to the English throne his first task was a military one. He destroyed the castles of the rebel barons, who had turned Stephen's reign into confusion, and subdued the rebellious Scots. He restored efficient government and tax collection, and as well as reviving the royal law courts, he introduced the system of trial by jury in place of barbaric trials by ordeal or combat. He then had to take his army to France for similar work there.

In 1162 the King took a step which led to the events that were to make his reign famous – or infamous – for centuries to come. He had a friend and adviser Thomas Becket appointed Archbishop of Canterbury. To his dismay and anger, Becket turned out to be obstinate and much too independent for his liking. Whenever there were clashes between the Church's wishes and those of the King, Becket was vigorously on the side of the Church. Within two years matters came to a head when

Becket refused to agree to various rights over the now wealthy and powerful Church which, by custom, the King had always held. Henry seized his property as punishment and Becket fled to France. There he remained until 1170 when he returned – in a triumphal procession – arrogantly to excommunicate priests who had, at the King's bidding, taken over the Archbishop's function by crowning his eldest son Henry heir to the throne. This step was intended to guarantee Henry the crown later, without any of the disputes that had so often occurred at the successions of the quarrelsome Norman monarchs.

'Will no one rid me of this turbulent priest?' cried the King in a fury. His words were taken literally: four knights rode to Canterbury, and there stabbed Becket to death in his own cathedral. The spot still remains, although much of the cathedral was burnt down a few years later, and was rebuilt as we see it today in Gothic style. This dreadful murder sent a shudder of revulsion through all Christian countries. The martyred Becket was made a saint, his mischief-making quite forgotten; and Henry himself did penance on his knees, whipped by monks, for the crime. He had to give up most of his attempts to curb the power of the Church.

In spite of this, Henry's command over his huge empire remained as strong as ever, but not his command over his own children, who began quarrelling over what parts of his lands each would in due course inherit. Two of his sons died, leaving John his favourite, and Richard eyeing one another jealously. Richard got the wily King of France on his side and together they invaded Anjou. Treacherously, John joined them when he saw they were on the point of succeeding.

Already ill, and now broken-hearted at his sons' disloyalty, Henry, who was once so dominating and so energetic, lost the will to live. In one of his great castles on the river Loire he died and was buried at Fontevrault Abbey, like so many of his Plantagenet descendants.

Henry's long reign came at a time when all kinds of new ideas were in the air. It was the period when knights-errant wandered from court to court and tournament to tournament, and when scholars travelled the known world in pursuit of learning, especially new ideas in mathematics, astronomy and medicine. At this time Arabic numerals, which we use today, began to replace the clumsy Roman ones. Monasteries were

rapidly increasing in number in England, and many of them ran boys' schools, though only the rich could afford to send their sons to them.

Henry's court was famed for its enthusiasm for debating knotty problems, everyone was interested in knowledge and education, and with greater prosperity more people could afford to acquire them, even though two books (hand-written) might cost as much as a house. All this Henry encouraged and with it the development of a really sound system of justice that slowly grew into the law courts of today. Henry was renowned for his generosity to the poor and his willingness to talk with even the humblest of his subjects. The blot of Becket's murder is a small matter by comparison with all the valuable things that Henry achieved.

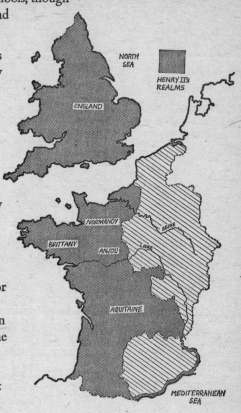

Richard I 1189–1199

Age 32–42. Son of Henry II. Married Berengaria (French).
No children. Killed in battle. Buried at Fontevrault (France).

Brave to the point of recklessness, tall, blond and athletic, Richard, known as Cœur-de-Lion, or Lionheart, was interested in only two things, tournaments and crusading. He spent less than a year in his own kingdom, which he used merely to raise money to pay for his expeditions. He once said, 'I would have sold London itself if I could have found a rich enough buyer.' Yet in the terrible famine of 1195, he gave free food to thousands in need.

The purpose of the Crusades, of which there were eight between 1095 and 1291, was to free Jerusalem and the Holy Land from the Turkish Saracens (Moslems) who occupied it. Thousands marched from Europe to fight, plunder, worship and massacre or be massacred. It was the Third Crusade (1190) that Richard led, during which he gained much ground from the Saracens though he failed to capture Jerusalem itself. Saladin was the unbeatable leader of the Saracens. He was a chivalrous man who even sent his enemy Richard a gift of fruit when he was ill with fever. As to Richard, he won his men's affection by rescuing the wounded from the enemy, and helping to haul the heavy siege catapults across the sun-scorched desert.

In 1192, on his way back from the Crusade, Richard's ship was wrecked in the Adriatic Sea. Wearing disguise he set off across Europe, but was captured by the Duke of Austria and then sold to the German Emperor who imprisoned him in a castle for over a year. The story is told that his favourite minstrel, Blondel, went from castle to castle in the guise of a wandering troubadour to seek the music-loving King.

To raise a ransom of £100,000, his English subjects handed over a quarter of all their possessions, the churches sold their gold plate and the monasteries gave all the wool from their flocks of sheep.

During Richard's absence, his envious brother John had been plotting with the King of France, and they had seized some of Richard's castles in Normandy. It took Richard five years of fighting to get them all back, and in the last battle he was killed by a bolt from a crossbow. In his will he left all he had to various religious causes and charities. Slight though his contact with England had been, his heroism made him one of the most popular kings.

Heraldry became well established in his time. Richard's shield bore the gold lions on a red background which are still part of the royal coat of arms today.

John 1199—1216

Age about 32–49. Son of Henry II. Married Isabel (English)
then Isabella (French). Five children. Buried at Worcester.

Treacherous John, plump and curly-haired, was so incompetent in war
that after he came to the throne he lost both Normandy and Anjou to the
King of France and earned the nickname Soft Sword. So for the first
time since 1066, England became the principal kingdom and not a mere
appendage to realms in France.

John blundered too in his dealings with the Church. The Pope had
nominated Stephen Langton as Archbishop of Canterbury in 1205.
When John tried to oppose this because he wanted to nominate a friend
of his own, the Pope excommunicated him and after nine years of
defiance he had to give in. During these long years the whole country
lay under an interdict: that is, the Pope forbade church services and even
the burial of the dead in holy ground. John's subjects felt this meant
eternal damnation for their souls, and they bitterly blamed John.

Things might have gone differently. John had a young nephew Arthur,
Prince of Brittany, son of his dead eldest brother, who claimed to be the
rightful heir to the English crown. In 1202 the King of France found an
excuse to invade Normandy and give the sixteen-year-old Arthur many
of the lands that were rightly John's. Incensed at this, John gave battle
and took Arthur prisoner. He was held in a fortress in Normandy and no
more was ever heard of him. John had had him murdered, but exactly
when and how was never known. Not even this savage crime saved the
situation for John: Normandy remained in French hands.

John added to his unpopularity by greedily taxing the people. Eventually
barons and clergy united to insist that he agree to a 'great charter'
(written in Latin on parchment) guaranteeing justice, fair taxes and the
Church's freedom to appoint its officials. Magna Carta, as it was called,
was sealed on the banks of the Thames at Runnymede (near Windsor) in
the summer of 1215. But within a year John began to break the promises
he had made. The barons rose in revolt against him. Galloping from
place to place in the course of this civil war, John took a short cut across
the sands of the Wash just when the tide was coming in fast. The horses
with his baggage were submerged, and his crown and other jewels

were swept out to sea. Worse was to come, for John fell ill a few days later and died, asking with his last breath to be buried at Worcester. He was one of England's most unpopular kings. 'No man may ever trust him,' said a writer of that time, 'for his heart is soft and cowardly.' John was capable of furious rages – 'his eyes darted fire and his face became livid'. He could be cruel, greedy and moody. But he could also be merciful and generous, was very well read and hard-working, and he gave fair judgments. When his servants became old or ill, he saw that they had good care. He enjoyed whiling away the time with backgammon, flirting and wine, and he took more baths than most people at that time – about one a month! And he did achieve some good things for England. He was the first king to organize a navy. He was clever and firm when it came to organizing tax-collection and administering the law. He gave the growing towns charters which made them independent of the barons, and allowed them to elect their own mayors to run their own courts and markets. He also gave a lot of help and advice when London Bridge (1202) and the port of Liverpool (1207) were being built. Perhaps John was not quite so black as he is painted.

1216   1220

Henry III 1216—1272

Age 9–65. Son of John. Married Eleanor (French). Six children. Buried in Westminster Abbey.

London being in the hands of the French, the boy king had to be crowned at Gloucester, with his mother's coronet, since the crown of England had been lost by his father John. Few barons were present, there was little show and no banquet.

At first Henry was too young to rule, but he had good men to do so in his place. Soon the French invaders were driven out and Henry had a proper coronation in Westminster Abbey.

When he did start to rule he proved to be a weak king, good company but untrustworthy and given to tantrums. Heavy taxation of his subjects, expensive but unsuccessful military expeditions in Europe, unpopular and greedy French courtiers (his wife's relatives), costly buildings and clothes and jewels, and broken promises to improve his ways meant that as the years passed he became heartily disliked.

By 1258 rebellion was simmering and its leader was an arrogant Frenchman, Simon de Montfort. Once he had been so much a favourite that in 1238 he had married the King's sister. But since then the two men had quarrelled repeatedly. When the discontented barons turned to Simon to lead them in their struggle against the extravagant King he saw a chance for advancing his own fortunes.

It seemed success would be his when, at the battle of Lewes (Sussex) in 1264, he took the King prisoner and forced him to agree that from then on he would take the advice of a council composed of two men from each shire and each big town in England. (The proclamation of this was issued in English, whereas ever since the Norman Conquest such documents had been in French.) Perhaps even Simon had no idea how important this new step would turn out to be; it was to lead to the House of Commons that we have today, with elected representatives from every part of Britain. A year later, however, all was over for Simon. Henry's loyal son Prince Edward came to his father's rescue, and at the battle of Evesham (Worcestershire), with the sky darkened by a summer storm, he killed Simon de Montfort and hacked off his head.

From then on Edward took over many of the affairs of state from his father, who was well content to spend his remaining years on matters that interested him more – and which were of lasting benefit to England. For although Henry III may have been a failure in political matters, he was great in one thing. Because of his admiration for French architecture he gave tremendous support to schemes for similar buildings in England. As a result of his enthusiasm some of the loftiest cathedrals in decorated style were built, such as Westminster Abbey (the original Norman abbey had been burned down), and the most impressive parts of Wells, Peterborough, Lincoln and Salisbury cathedrals. In these buildings pointed arches, slender columns, soaring spires, leafy carvings, handsome tombs and elaborate shrines, often painted and gilded, all combined to make a new style that was unlike the simplicity of the century before. Castles and halls too were improved and colourfully decorated. Tiles, furniture, stained glass, tapestries, wall paintings, wood panelling, and sculpture adorned his buildings; and he knew and talked with the craftsmen who made these things for him. He loved clothes made from colourful silks, gilded leather shoes, and jewellery too. Once when the King asked the London merchants for money, they said he could sell them his jewels. He replied, 'If they are rich enough to buy all my jewels, they can afford to give me something freely!'

Henry also encouraged learning. During his reign, many wandering Franciscan and Dominican friars came to England, followers of the Italian St Francis and the Spanish St Dominic. They were content to live in poverty while preaching or serving others. They began teaching at the universities of Oxford and Cambridge, and to help them build colleges, Henry gave money, let them use timber from his forests, and gave them much encouragement.

Henry was generous. Old records still survive which list some of his gifts, such as hundreds of tunics, cloaks and shoes distributed to the poor each Christmas; money to a maidservant who had gone blind; a barrel of wine to a harper when his child was born; and a rabbit-fur tunic for his fiddler's wife. There were Christmas feasts for the poor in Windsor Castle, money to feed prisoners in Newgate on a feast day, money to build a hospital where women could go to have their babies, and gifts to friaries and abbeys.

1240

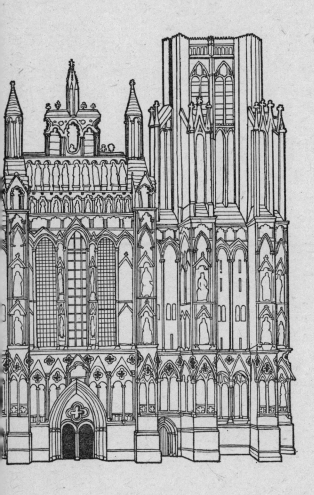

The wives of kings do not often play much part in history. But Henry's wife Eleanor did. She was perhaps England's most unpopular queen, despite her beauty and her elegance. She had come from the warm south of France and landed at Dover in the freezing winter of 1235 to meet her as yet unseen bridegroom; and they loved one another at first sight. Four hundred leading citizens of London, in cloth-of-gold tunics, had escorted her to her coronation in London through streets hung with silk banners. But from then on trouble began. With her had come a crowd of French relatives, intent on grabbing all they could, and the Queen helped them to do so. Some were even made bishops. The more they squandered the money given them by the King (and raised by taxing the people), the more hated became his French wife. When Henry was abroad, Eleanor ruled in his place. Her attempts to tax the citizens of London were resented, especially when she had the Lord Mayor thrown into prison until the money was paid. Once when sailing up the Thames she was pelted with filth by citizens crowding on the bridge above. Yet in spite of this, she and Henry and their children remained one of the happiest and most united of all England's royal families.

Edward I 1272–1307

Age 33–68. Son of Henry III. Married Eleanor (Spanish)
then Margaret (French). Eleven children. Buried in Westminster Abbey.

Edward was one of England's greatest kings. He was outstanding in
warfare, in justice and in governing the country. It was he who for the
first time brought together both the lords and the common people in
one great council, Parliament, and accepted that they should have a say
in what taxes might be collected. But he was tough and ruthless too.

He had been a happy child, living with his brothers and sisters in
handsome apartments his father had designed for them in Windsor
Castle, while his parents and the Court travelled ceaselessly from town
to town, as monarchs did in those days. When only fifteen he had been
married to the King of Spain's sixteen-year-old daughter. They came to
love each other very much, and when she died in Nottinghamshire
nearly forty years later he wrote, 'My harp is turned to mourning, in
life I loved her dearly, nor can I cease to love her in death.' Wherever her
coffin rested on its long journey back to London for burial, he had a cross
built in her memory; Eleanor crosses still stand at Geddington,
Northampton, Hardingstone, Waltham, Banbury, and outside Charing
Cross station in London – the last two are replicas.

When Edward came to the throne he was an exceptionally tall and
handsome young man, famous for his strength and skill in tournaments.
But he had a reputation for being rather a bully and too impetuous to be
reliable. He had won the battle of Evesham (see page 22) by what was
thought to be a rather shabby trick – luring Simon de Montfort to his
death by hoisting the banners of captive barons. He was also very savage
in punishing the rebels and seizing their property for himself and his
family. But all was forgiven and forgotten when he went on a four-year
crusade and made himself a reputation as 'the greatest lance in the world'.
It was while he was on his way home from this that he was sent word of
his father's death.

As soon as he returned, still deeply grieving, he had a magnificent gilded
tomb made for his father. Then he sent inspectors all over the country
to report back on what was going on. A lot was wrong. Under Henry

III's weak rule, officials in distant parts had seized the chance to feather their own nests by extorting money from local people. Edward put an end to this, and brought in laws to maintain order and fair play.

Soon, however, these activities were interrupted by uproar in Wales. Raiders from the northern parts such as Snowdon and Anglesey had been giving continual trouble, and although lords with castles in south Wales or on the Welsh borders were supposed to control these raiders, they often feuded among themselves instead. One of the Welshmen, Llewelyn ap Gruffydd, set himself up as the Prince of Wales. In 1277 Edward marched against him with a huge army of mounted knights plus archers on foot, and forced him to surrender. It was in this Welsh war that a revolutionary new weapon was used with deadly effect – the powerful longbow. Its arrows were capable of piercing the clanking chain-mail worn by the knights. This invention was as important in its way as the later invention of gunpowder. Edward took much of the land which Llewelyn had occupied, but he allowed him to go on calling himself Prince of Wales. This was a mistake, for five years later Llewelyn was plotting again. Once more Edward attacked. Llewelyn was killed in battle, his head was sent as a trophy to be paraded through London, and Edward took over the whole of Wales. In 1301 he made his son Prince of Wales, and all male heirs to the English throne have carried this title ever since.

To keep the country under control, he built a ring of spectacular castles which can still be visited today. They are different in style from the Norman ones, which had 'keeps' in the middle, and more like the crusaders' castles with their massive outer walls fortified with towers and gatehouses. Caernarvon, Conway, Harlech, Beaumaris and Caerphilly are among the castles he built.

A darker side to Edward's reign was to be found in his treatment of the Jews, whom he expelled from England so that he could seize their property and raise enough money to go on paying his huge army. For no sooner was Wales settled than Scotland gave trouble.

Although the Scots were largely independent, they recognized Edward as their overlord, but when they found his demands too heavy they rebelled in 1296. Edward's army moved in swiftly, sacked the rich port of Berwick, defeated the Scots at Dunbar, seized their sacred coronation stone from Scone Abbey and placed it in Westminster Abbey, where it still remains. This ruthless treatment aroused the most bitter hatred, and for years to come the Scots kept on carrying out guerrilla-style raids on the north of England. Among their brave leaders were men like William Wallace, who was eventually hanged, drawn and quartered at Tyburn, and after him, Robert Bruce. But much as the Scots hated Edward, his men were devoted to him. He shared their hardships, dressed plainly, and was ready to talk to anyone who brought a problem to him.

The King, now getting old, died on his way to attack the Scots yet again. With his last breath he commanded that his bones should be carried into battle until the last Scot had surrendered, but his wish was in vain. His nickname, Hammer of the Scots, which is on his tomb, was well deserved, and for centuries to come the slaughter and destruction which he had started continued to damage both countries.

Edward was a loving, if tyrannical, father; at his daughter's wedding he lost his temper over something and threw her coronet into the fire! His accounts show many details of toys he gave his children, such as model castles and boats. He enjoyed chess and other games, jokes, hawking, reading and listening to the music of his various minstrels. He had the first accurate and detailed map of England drawn. When a body said to be that of King Arthur was discovered at Glastonbury, he helped to carry the coffin to its reburial. He sent explorers and traders to Persia and beyond. There have been few kings with so wide a range of interests and so many great achievements.

Edward II 1307–1327

Age 23–43. Son of Edward I. Married Isabella (French). Four children.
Murdered. Buried in Gloucester Cathedral.

Outwardly Edward II was as tall and good-looking as his father, but he cared nothing for the duties of a king which had so absorbed his father. He used the position simply to enrich his favourites and to lead a life of pleasure. Strangely, this sometimes included working like a peasant – digging, thatching and farming.

He gave up the Scottish war, leaving Robert Bruce triumphant, and returned to London for a life of frivolity. He gave his favourite, Piers Gaveston (a French knight), an earldom that had in the past been reserved for the sons of kings, married Gaveston to his niece and, shockingly, took from his own bride (the sixteen-year-old Isabella) many of her jewels and wedding gifts and loaded Gaveston with them. Arrogant Gaveston, dressing himself in royal purple, sneered at and ridiculed the infuriated lords. Within a year the nobles got together and insisted that Edward dismiss his favourite. He agreed, but after a few months Gaveston was back at court again. Some of the lords then acted swiftly; Gaveston was seized and beheaded.

Among the discontented lords was Edward's own nephew, the mighty Earl of Lancaster, with his huge private army. When Edward sought his aid in a renewed attempt to subdue the Scots, Lancaster refused, and Robert Bruce, with a small force of spearmen, completely defeated the vast English army of cavalry and archers at the battle of Bannockburn (1314).

By now Edward was little more than a puppet in England, while Lancaster did as he pleased and feuds raged between the barons. To make life even more wretched for the people, there occurred floods that ruined the crops, and during the worst famine Europe has ever known, 'the poor ate dogs, the dung of doves, and even their own children'.

The King had not, it seemed, learned his lesson from the Gaveston affair, for within a few years he once more started giving land and money to a new young favourite, Hugh Despenser and his father, both of them lords from the Welsh borders. Once more the other jealous barons demanded the exile of these favourites, but this time Edward fought back. Lancaster's army was defeated, his head was hacked off and Edward, with the Despensers, was left in power. Among Lancaster's followers had been the real Robin Hood, later outlawed for joining the rebel forces.

But one person had not been reckoned with – Isabella the Queen, who had been humiliated by having her jewellery snatched away to adorn the beloved Gaveston, and who had equal cause to hate Hugh Despenser. One of the rebel lords, Mortimer, became her lover and the two began to plot the King's downfall. Together with her fourteen-year-old son Edward, they led an army, hanged the two Despensers, imprisoned the King and forced him to abdicate in favour of his son.

The deposed King was kept, half starving, in a dungeon in Berkeley Castle (Gloucestershire), until Mortimer ordered his gaolers to murder Edward by thrusting a red-hot poker into his body – a terrible death.

Perhaps Edward should not be blamed for his failure. His mother had died when he was only six, and his father was too busy with state affairs to have much time for the lonely boy. Although he grew up unfitted to be a king, he could have been a good country squire. He was the first king to encourage the theatre, and to write poetry. His tragedy was that he inherited a kingdom he could not control.

Edward III 1327–1377

Age 15–65. Son of Edward II. Married Philippa (Flemish).
Eleven children. Buried in Westminster Abbey.

The young king had had a disturbed childhood. He knew how
unpopular his father had been, and how unhappy his mother. Some of
the guilt for his father's death lay on him. His reign began in a state of
strife, and because he was so young, the country was under the control of
Mortimer and his father's enemies.

As soon as he was able, he arrested Mortimer, sending men through a
secret passage into Nottingham Castle to surprise him in his bedroom
there, and had him hanged. His mother he sent into retirement at Castle
Rising, Norfolk.

His was to be a very long reign indeed, covering half a century of change.
In spite of its uneasy start, it was to prove to be a notable reign and
Edward grew to be a magnificent king who inspired the loyalty of all the
barons. They were heartened when he achieved one military success
after another, his banquets and pageantry delighted them and he
captured their imagination with his new ideas of chivalry. It was he who
founded the select band of twenty-six Knights of the Garter. The story
goes that when a lady, later to marry his son, the Black Prince, dropped
her garter, he picked it up, saying to the sniggering courtiers, 'Evil be to
him who evil thinks', and made this the motto of the Knights of the
Garter. He made George the national saint of England and dedicated
to him the superb chapel which he rebuilt for the Garter knights inside
Windsor Castle. He arranged spectacular tournaments, with knights
jousting in single combat – earlier combats were more like mock battles.

Early in his reign the young King defeated the Scots completely. They
turned to France for help. This was dangerous for England as she now
controlled only a tiny remnant of the French possessions that had once
been hers. The King of France, therefore, would be delighted for any
excuse to get hold of this too, and perhaps some part of England as well
if he got the chance. Edward believed the best defence would be to attack,
and by luck an opportunity arose. In 1328 the King of France died
without a son. Edward, as his nephew, had some claim to the French
throne, although in fact it was Philippe VI, a cousin, who succeeded to it.

1340

Edward had not been strong enough to contest the claim at the time, but ten years later he invaded France via Flanders to assert his rights. This was the beginning of the so-called Hundred Years War (1338–1453) which was to continue on and off throughout five reigns, exhausting both nations.

At first Edward made little progress except for one victory at Sluys in 1340 when, after nine hours fighting 'right furious and horrible', he scattered the fleet sent to prevent him crossing the Channel. But later things changed. Edward landed in Normandy in 1346 and marched across the country to join up with his forces already in Flanders, burning and destroying as he went. Only when he had got as far as Crécy did the French send their huge army to meet him. It was at sunset on a hot August day when battle began. The English archers with their deadly longbows (see page 29) 'stepped forth one pace and let fly their arrows so wholly together and so thick it seemed to snow'. By midnight thousands of Frenchmen and horses, with arrows still piercing them, lay dead in heaps upon the ground.

Edward and his army marched on to besiege the port of Calais. This he did for a whole year until he starved its stubborn and courageous people into surrender.

Before the year was out, the Scots too were beaten when they tried to take advantage of Edward's absence to invade the north of England, and their king was taken to the Tower of London as a prisoner.

Although there had been a truce after Crécy, when Philippe VI was succeeded by King Jean fighting was renewed. This time it was the Black Prince, Edward's son, who led the English to another famous victory at Poitiers (1356). At this battle the French King was captured and sent to London to join the Scottish King in the Tower until a ransom equal to nearly one million pounds could be paid for him. After a few more years' fighting, the French gave in to most of Edward's claims; he got nearly a quarter of France, though he agreed to give up any right to the French throne.

But meantime another invincible enemy had arisen – the Black Death, which first reached England in 1347. This was bubonic plague which, starting in China, was carried by rats throughout Europe, killing one person in every three, and among them Edward's beloved queen, Philippa. Skin blotches and swellings, delirium and insanity, led swiftly to death. The corpses were shovelled into huge pits as there were too many for individual graves to be dug. These were years of famine too, adding to the general misery and terror. Those who could afford to do so, paid money to the churches for 'chantries' – regular prayers to be said for their souls after their all-too-likely deaths from the plague. For several years the plague still raged, and took a toll of Edward's fighting men, who were now too few to defend the French towns and castles which had been so hard won. By 1374, England held only Calais in the north and a tiny strip of land in the south.

At home the Black Death had created such a shortage of craftsmen and even of men to harvest the corn, that laws were passed to keep down wages and food prices; and taxes were reduced because of the poverty that followed on the heels of the plague.

The once great King was now ageing. Even before his wife died he had turned to the company of Alice Perrers, a scheming woman who used every opportunity and cheating method to enrich herself. It is even said that she snatched the rings from his fingers as soon as he had died. Parliament took vigorous steps to curb her activities in 1376, but this brought swift retaliation from Edward's powerful younger son, John of Gaunt, now Duke of Lancaster.

Because his first son, the Black Prince, had died that same year (his tomb and armour are in Canterbury Cathedral), the people began to fear that John of Gaunt might try to seize the throne at Edward's death. However, it did go to the rightful heir, grandson Richard, son of the Black Prince.

During Edward III's long reign, much occurred to change the English way of life for the better, in spite of wars, the heavy taxation war caused, and the dreadful plague. Parliament, divided into two Houses, Lords and Commons, met regularly. Law enforcement was improved. Merchants traded busily with other countries. Learning spread, and so did art; this was the great age of brilliant wall-paintings and illuminated manuscripts.

It was also the time of Wyclif and his followers, called Lollards, who were fierce critics of the corruption and pride now spreading through the Catholic Church. The Lollards preached sermons against the power of the Pope, urging people to return to more spiritual ways with less striving after wealth. Wyclif had the Latin Bible translated into English for the first time, so that even ill-educated people might understand it. Wyclif was in a way the first Protestant.

The land itself was changing too, as gradually marshes were drained and the great wild forests were turned into fields of crops. At last a way was found to harness oxen or horses to ploughs and so more land could be cultivated. It is known that the climate too changed, but for the worse. No longer could grapes, for instance, be grown in England.

Just over three centuries have now gone by since William the Conqueror became king and life is far more rich and complex. London's population has grown so much that houses spread out beyond the city's defensive walls, and the riverside is lined with bishops' palaces. Every night the curfew bell still rings to warn people outside when the city gates are about to close, and every morning the gates open so that food for the markets can be brought in, together with wool, cloth, charcoal and wood, pottery, and other necessities. Merchants are now becoming as important as knights and barons, their houses rich with tapestries, silver and alabaster carvings. There are now eighty-eight guilds – associations to look after all the different crafts and trades in London. The court, government, Parliament and the lawyers are more or less settled in London, and not continually moving from town to town. At the Tower of London armourers equip the knights and archers for wars abroad, and the Royal Mint turns out gold nobles and silver groats to pay them. Pageants and banquets are frequent and the courtiers who attend these wear brilliant colours and valuable furs in new fashions tailored to fit the shape of the body – far more elaborate than the simple tunics of 1066.

No longer is it just the clergy who can read and write. But the Church is still as important as in William's day; and now London is a forest of a hundred Gothic church spires, while just outside the city stand many large abbeys and priories in elegant style.

With all this development the feudal system is passing away and the power of the barons with it, as trade and the towns take on a new importance in medieval history.

Richard II 1377–1399

*Age 10–32. Grandson of Edward III. Married Anne (Bohemian)
then Isabella (French). No children. Murdered.
Buried in Westminster Abbey.*

Sheer hunger and poverty caused the Peasants' Revolt led by Wat Tyler
in 1381. Hordes of angry Kentish peasants advanced on the city of
London, set its wooden houses ablaze and killed the Archbishop of
Canterbury. Young Richard rode out to Mile End together with some of
his nobles to meet Wat Tyler face to face, and he agreed to the peasants'
demands – low rents and an end to serfdom, which was the system under
which peasants were obliged to work for the same lord no matter how
badly they were treated. But not all the peasants were satisfied with this
and so another meeting was arranged at Smithfield. There impetuous
barons killed Wat Tyler. The rebels began to raise their longbows, but
the fourteen-year-old king, tall and fair-haired, rode towards them
crying, 'Sirs, will you kill your king? I am your king, and your leader!'
The peasants went home, but the king did not keep his promises.

Richard, having arranged a truce with France, turned to a life of
extravagance and pleasure, surrounded by idle favourites. He tried to
turn the clock back by dismissing Parliament and executing or exiling
his enemies.

Richard and his court deliberately dressed in a luxurious way to impress
all visitors with royal pomp and the importance of the King. Lords and
commoners alike were expected to kneel at the foot of the high throne
on which he seated himself. He built up a fearsome army of his own,
dressed in tunics with his badge – a white hart – still seen on inn signs.
He believed his power as king was given by God.

Not surprisingly, many people began to wish the country had a better
ruler and some thoughts turned to John of Gaunt, although he too had
been unpopular. But John remained loyal to the King.

When John of Gaunt died, the greedy King seized all his vast estates.
John's son, Henry, who now became Duke of Lancaster, raised
an army to assert his rights, and Richard did not stand a chance.

Parliament speedily elected Henry king while Richard languished in prison. But when, a year later, some of Richard's friends tried unsuccessfully to assassinate Henry and release Richard, it seemed too risky to let the deposed King live on, so he was secretly murdered, possibly starved to death, in Pontefract Castle, and buried in a common grave at Kings Langley in Hertfordshire. Years later Henry V had his bones reburied in Westminster Abbey.

Had Richard not sought absolute power he might have made a fine king.

He encouraged artists and architects such as the builder of Westminster Hall, and it was at his suggestion that Chaucer wrote the *Canterbury Tales*, in English and not the French of the Normans. He cared not only about fine clothes but about cleanliness too; it was he who invented the handkerchief, and at his table food was eaten with spoons and not fingers. In his palaces baths and lavatories were provided. One of the earliest cookery books was written at his orders. He did much to make English life more civilized.

Henry IV 1399–1413

*Age 32–46. Grandson of Edward III. Married Mary (English)
then Joan (French). Six children. Died of leprosy.
Buried in Canterbury Cathedral.*

Short and red-haired, Henry was the first truly *English* king of England,
but many people resented being ruled by a usurper. The first revolt was
savagely put down: rebel corpses were chopped up and carried to
London in sacks. In a panic Henry had Richard murdered (see page 39).
To end rumours that Richard still lived, Henry had his decaying body
dug up and put on view in London.

The Welsh, led by Owen Glendower, then took the opportunity to
rebel and the Scots gave trouble too: it took Henry most of his short
reign to restore order. The French King refused to recognize Henry as
King of England, referring to him always as 'that lord'. Trade between
England and France almost stopped. Persecution of the Lollards (see page
36) became worse: many were burnt alive. All this and his guilty
conscience weighed heavily on Henry, and when he fell ill with leprosy
he believed this was God's punishment for his sins. He wrote a will
asking to be buried next to England's holiest saint, Thomas Becket,
hoping this would help him to get to heaven.

A strange story is told about
Henry's death. It had been
foretold that he would die in
Jerusalem, so he thought he was
safe in England. But when
visiting Westminster Abbey he
collapsed and was carried to
the abbot's room and there
died. This room was called the
Jerusalem Chamber.

Henry V 1413—1422

Age 26–35. Son of Henry IV. Married Catherine (French). One child. Buried in Westminster Abbey.

Henry was so skilled in military affairs that he nearly became King of France. His first tremendous victory was at the battle of Agincourt (1415). He ruthlessly besieged one town after another and when the starving women and children left Rouen, he would not let them pass and 12,000 perished. When at last the French sought peace, Henry was able to dictate terms. He persuaded the French King to let him marry his daughter and become heir to the French throne. But Henry died only two years later.

Lean-faced and serious, Henry was not only a great war leader but a man of outstanding piety, justice and energy too. During the years of battling in France, he regularly had sent on to him all the petitions his subjects sent to London. He lived for his work and his wars, with little time for home-life or other pleasures – except composing and listening to music.

1413   1420

Henry VI 1422—1461

Age 1–40. Son of Henry V. Married Margaret (French). One child. Murdered. Buried in Windsor Castle.

The story of this sad reign involves two deeply religious people, very different from one another and on opposite sides in the war. Both were in the end imprisoned and killed. One was Joan of Arc and the other Henry VI himself.

For the first twenty years of Henry's reign, it was his uncles and others who governed for him in England and also in France, which he had inherited under the treaty which his victorious father had made in 1420. Among these men was the Duke of Suffolk, who used his position to enrich himself while neglecting justice and order in the country. After many years of enduring this state of affairs, the peasants of Kent rose up in a revolt, known after their leader as Cade's Rebellion (1450). The King bravely rode out among them, not to fight but to speak peaceably with them. But when, after entering London, the mob became violent, the Londoners drove them out and killed Cade.

In France there was far worse trouble, with war continuing for many years because the French had no intention of being ruled by England no matter what the treaty of 1420 had said. The lords who ruled on Henry's behalf would not yield an inch, however, and so the war dragged on.

The French were losing when a peasant girl, Joan of Arc, made her way to the castle where the Dauphin, heir to the French throne, had his court. She claimed she had seen visions and had a call from God to restore the Dauphin to the throne. Of course the courtiers scoffed, until Joan unhesitatingly recognized the Dauphin when he stood disguised among them to test her powers. Joan was given command of the French armies and, dressed in armour like a man, led them to victory after victory. But then success turned to disaster and she became a prisoner of the English, who brought against her a charge of practising witchcraft. In 1421 she was burnt alive in the streets of Rouen. Later she was made a saint and there is a statue of her in Winchester Cathedral.

1440

By 1453, English possessions in France had once more been reduced to Calais, and a French king ruled again. At long last the Hundred Years War was over.

At home, however, there was to be no peace. There were still many barons who resented the way the Lancaster family had seized the throne back in 1399 and did not think that Henry IV, V or VI were rightful kings. According to them, the York family, cousins of the Lancasters, were truly entitled to reign, and they were dissatisfied with the way those now in power were running the country. Because the Lancaster emblem was a red rose and the York emblem a white one, the struggle for power which now started was known as the Wars of the Roses. They were to last even longer than the Hundred Years War.

Matters had become troubled when in 1454 the King had had a mental breakdown which made him incapable of ruling. As the King's son was only an infant, his cousin the Duke of York was appointed Regent to rule on his behalf. When the King recovered, the Yorkists were unwilling to let him rule again. Battle was joined between their forces and his in the streets of St Albans (Hertfordshire) and the King was taken prisoner while sheltering inside a shop.

It happened that the King had married a particularly courageous and quick-tempered French princess called Margaret, who was a much tougher personality than himself, and she was not going to tolerate this state of affairs. She assembled an army and in 1460 fought a battle at Wakefield (Yorkshire) and another at St Albans in 1461. On both occasions the Yorkists were massacred, and at Wakefield Richard, Duke of York was killed. Margaret had the Duke's head put on a pikestaff, mockingly adorned it with a paper crown and displayed it on the gates of the city of York.

Her success was brief. For now a formidable young man, Edward, became Duke of York in his father's place and, together with the Earl of Warwick, led the Yorkists in renewed attacks on the Lancastrians. In a heavy snowstorm at Towton (Yorkshire) he completely defeated them; the gale blew back the Lancastrian arrows and the snowflakes blinded them, but for six hours they stood until they could fight no more. The young Duke then deposed Henry and was crowned as Edward IV in his place. While Edward planned his coronation, the family of Henry

VI fled for their lives and faced bitter hardship as they hid in the forests and valleys of the North before finally escaping. For days all they had to eat was a herring each. Once, Queen Margaret was caught by Yorkist soldiers and nearly beheaded, but she persuaded a young squire to take her and her son up on his horse and off into the forest to hide. After making some final efforts to hold out in Bamburgh and other northern castles, they had to give up, defeated by the pounding of Edward's cannons. At last they arrived in France with nothing but the clothes they were wearing.

Henry still remained in hiding in the Pennines and was found there by Yorkists a year later. With his feet tied to the stirrups of a horse, and a straw hat instead of a crown, he was led to the Tower of London.

Henry's mental breakdowns were hardly surprising in such a life of strain. As a child he hardly knew his father or, indeed, his mother as she remarried and went away. As an adult he was dominated by powerful uncles and other advisers. Two outstanding women, Joan of Arc and his wife, led armies while he was a mere puppet in other men's power. Although he was a peace-lover, the first half of his reign was dominated by the last stages of the Hundred Years War and the second half by the start of the Wars of the Roses.

Henry VI would probably have made an excellent priest and might even perhaps have been worthy of sainthood, but he was not an effective king. He was very religious, truthful and generous to the poor, and often spared the lives of criminals. He even pardoned a man who, during one of his imprisonments, wounded him, merely saying, 'Forsooth, you do foully to smite an anointed king so.'

He gave money to build two superb colleges, Eton at Windsor and King's at Cambridge. Unlike many kings, he dressed very simply in a long black gown and hood, with plain boots rather like a farmer's. Sometimes he wore a scratchy hair shirt as a self-punishment. He was prudish and frowned on flirting or similar behaviour at his court. What he thought about being king is summed up in this verse which he wrote:

Kingdoms are but cares.
State is devoid of stay.
Riches are ready snares,
And hasten to decay.

Edward IV 1461–1483

Age 19–41. Great-great-great-grandson of Edward III.
Married Elizabeth (English). Nine children.
Buried in Windsor Castle.

For nine years Edward managed to hold on to the throne (1461–70) but gradually the Earl of Warwick, his former ally, was turning against him. Edward had not rewarded him as he had hoped, but instead had given a lot of power to the Queen and her family, the Woodvilles. The discontented Warwick started to plot with Margaret in France. His daughter and her son (rightful heir to the throne after Henry) were married. In 1470 Warwick led an invasion and briefly restored Henry to the throne, but Warwick himself held on to all the power. Edward fled from King's Lynn to Holland.

That winter, however, Edward returned from his exile in Holland, landing in the north of England with a fresh army including 'black and smoky gunners' from Flanders. Battle was joined at Barnet in the mists before dawn. Edward's army 'advanced banners, did blow up trumpets, and set upon them; first with shot and then, and soon, they joined and came to hand-strokes'. There, and at the later battle of Tewkesbury, the Lancastrians were defeated. Not only Warwick but Henry's seventeen-year-old son was killed, and his Queen, Margaret, was taken captive. Edward rode triumphantly into London in a procession of 'nobles, knights, and a host of horsemen larger than had ever been seen before', including the carriage of the captive Queen. As to Henry himself, he was at once taken to the Tower of London and there murdered, possibly by Richard, Duke of Gloucester (about him, more later). Henry's body was not buried as befitted a king but was taken to an abbey at Chertsey (Surrey). Only later was it reburied at Windsor.

Even as a boy, handsome Edward had been fond of rich clothes. There is a letter from him to his father asking for 'some fine bonnets', and thanking him for 'green gowns now late sent unto us to our great comfort'. Now that he had secured the throne he could have all he wanted. Six feet tall, a good dancer and huntsman, with beautiful manners and handwriting, he was popular with the ladies.

One in particular attracted him, Elizabeth Woodville, and the two had been married, secretly at first because Edward's advisers were pressing him to marry a foreign princess. The people welcomed Elizabeth warmly, decorating London Bridge with statues and bringing minstrels to play and pipe.

Edward was a good businessman and believed in peace rather than the glories of war. He himself did a lot of trading in wool, England's biggest export at the time. He was quick to realize the value of a new invention such as printing, which Caxton brought to England in 1476. Edward started a postal system with relays of horsemen carrying letters, and he encouraged much fine new building, including rebuilding the chapel in Windsor Castle, which he planned to hold the tombs of all future kings.

But there was a dark side to his character too. He was the first English king to use torture as a means of extracting confessions from spies, he had bribes paid to juries to convict people he wanted to see punished, he executed traitors by having them stuck on spikes, while even his brother, Clarence, was killed for treason – by being drowned in a barrel of wine.

Although Edward left the country secure and prosperous when he died suddenly from appendicitis, he also left it a problem. His son, the heir to the throne, was only a boy and doubts were cast on his right to reign.

Edward V 1483

Age 12. Son of Edward IV. Murdered in the Tower of London.
Now buried in Westminster Abbey.

Richard III 1483–1485

Age 31–33. Brother of Edward IV. Married Anne (English). One child.
Killed in battle 1485. Buried in Greyfriars Church, Leicester.

Sinister but probably untrue rumours surrounded Richard's early years.
Was it he who had killed Henry VI, Henry's son, and even his own
brother, the Duke of Clarence? (See previous reigns.) Worse still, was
it he who later ordered the murder of Edward IV's young sons, heirs to
the throne, so that he might wear the crown himself?

Richard had been completely loyal to Edward IV, his elder brother,
helping to lead his armies to victory, and later keeping order and justice
in the north of England. Edward IV had said in his will that until his son
grew up Richard should be Protector of England.

But Edward IV's scheming widow had other ideas. In April 1483 she
hurriedly had her twelve-year-old son brought to London to be crowned
Edward V. Richard, however, kidnapped him on the way and both he
and his younger brother were locked in the Tower of London while
Richard sent a message to his Yorkshire followers: 'Come unto us to
London, there to aid us against the Queen and her bloody adherents.'

His advisers meanwhile told him that he had a better claim to the throne
than Prince Edward, whose parents, they said, had not been properly
married – so in July Richard was crowned. Soon after, the two Princes in
the Tower were seen for the last time. What had been their fate? Two
hundred years later, their hidden bones were found by workmen
repairing a staircase in the Tower – proof of murder.

Trouble followed Richard. He had to put down revolts, his son and then
his wife died and finally an obscure Welshman called Henry Tudor, the
last of the Lancastrian family, *and* engaged to Edward V's sister Elizabeth
of York, claimed that he had a better right to the throne. He gathered an
army against Richard. At the battle of Bosworth (Leicestershire) in 1485
Richard, always brave, led a cavalry charge against Henry but was slain.
His crown rolled under a bush, to be picked up by the victorious Henry.

Henry VII 1485–1509

Age 28–52. Great-great-great-grandson of Edward III.
Married Elizabeth (daughter of Edward IV). Seven children.
Buried in Westminster Abbey.

Through Lancastrian Henry's marriage to the beautiful Princess Elizabeth of York, the wars of the red and the white roses at last came to an end.

Henry was troubled by rebels and by two impostors who tried to take Henry's crown from him. The first was Lambert Simnel, a young labourer who posed as a nephew of Edward IV and led a rebellion in 1487. His followers actually crowned him King Edward VI in Ireland (hearing this, King Henry said, 'The Irish will even crown apes').

The second impostor was Perkin Warbeck, an apprentice who claimed to be one of the royal Princes who had vanished mysteriously in the Tower of London four years before. He had himself crowned at Bodmin, Cornwall, and for years harassed Henry with armies he managed to raise.

Both revolts were crushed. Simnel was contemptuously put to work in the King's kitchens, turning the spit on which the sides of beef were roasted; Warbeck was executed.

Henry was a strong king who kept the quarrelsome barons in order, taxing and fining them heavily. He was the best businessman who ever reigned in England. He had spies in every country. To be sure of peace with Spain and Scotland he married his eldest son Arthur to a Spanish princess (Catherine of Aragon), and one of his daughters to the Scottish King. Arthur died within a year; but his sister's marriage was to have great consequences for British history a hundred years later. Trade prospered, and so did seafaring. John Cabot set sail and discovered Newfoundland in 1496. (Columbus had sailed from Spain to America four years before.) Much money was spent on ships for a great navy.

Playing-cards were invented early in Henry's reign: the queens in every pack represent Elizabeth of York, correctly shown holding a white rose.

It was Henry who built the red-brick palace at Richmond (Surrey) which was the first notable Tudor building. He also built the splendid chapel in Westminster Abbey that contains his gilded tomb – above this stands the red dragon of Wales, his homeland, while Henry's feet rest on the gold lion of England.

He founded the Yeomen of the Guard, on whose red tunics is still worn the Tudor rose, which combines the York and Lancaster roses in one emblem. His court was dazzling, with jewels and jesters, minstrels and pet leopards. A canopy was carried over him whenever he walked outdoors.

Although Henry got his crown by force and was never popular, he was respected by other monarchs, and even more than the York kings, he brought real progress to England, which now began moving out of the Middle Ages into a new period called the Renaissance, meaning re-birth.

Henry VIII 1509–1547

Age 18–56. Son of Henry VII. Married Catherine of Aragon (Spanish),
Anne Boleyn (English), Jane Seymour (English),
Anne of Cleves (Flemish–Belgian), Catherine Howard (English),
Catherine Parr (English). Three children. Buried in Windsor Castle.

Henry is famous for his six wives (two were divorced, two were
beheaded, one died and one outlived him), and for his quarrel with the
Pope which led to the start of the Protestant Church of England.

Tall, handsome, fashionable, learned, musical, athletic and above all
ambitious, young Henry was greedy for glory. He started his reign in a
very different style from his serious father with banquets and
tournaments, and then achieved two military successes. He invaded
France to help the Pope in a war against the French, where his army won
the battle of the Spurs, so-called because of the speed of the cavalry. At
home his armies marched on the Scots, who had invaded England, and
beat them at Flodden Field (1513), killing their king and many of their
nobles. Later Henry had a 'summit' meeting with the King of France in
an attempt to make peace. Because of the sumptuous clothes worn at this
month-long succession of banquets and jousting, it became known as the
Field of the Cloth of Gold.

At this time Luther, a German priest, was denouncing the Catholic
church for its luxury and idleness. Henry wrote a book in 1521 attacking
Luther's ideas, and the Pope rewarded him with the title Defender of the
Faith which British monarchs still carry (the letters F.D. on coins refer to
this) even though, a few years later, Henry quarrelled with the Pope.

The cause of the quarrel was a personal one. After nearly twenty years of
contented marriage, Catherine, who had been his brother Arthur's
widow, had failed to produce a son. So Henry wanted to divorce her,
attractive and intelligent though she was, and marry Anne Boleyn, so
much gayer and more elegant, and with whom he had fallen in love. The
Pope refused to give permission for a divorce, and even the powerful
Cardinal Wolsey, Henry's adviser, could not persuade him. Henry was
furious. He dismissed Wolsey, divorced Catherine and married Anne,
and set himself up in place of the Pope as supreme head of the Church in

1520

England. In addition, he ordered copies of the Bible in English (not Latin, as in the Catholic Church) to be used. In 1536 he began to destroy all the rich Catholic monasteries and to help himself to their wealth. This is why so many monastic ruins are to be seen today. He had already seized for his own use the palace Wolsey had built for himself, Hampton Court. Henry built many palaces too, including St James's, where his initial and Anne's can be seen on the brick tower.

Like Catherine, Anne bore only one child – another daughter. And so within three years Henry was casting about for some way to rid himself of her too. She was accused of having lovers and, as this would have been treason, was beheaded in the Tower of London in 1536. A few days later, Henry married modest Jane Seymour. She died in childbirth but gave Henry the son he wanted so much.

For some years Henry, now middle-aged and fat, lived alone. But in 1540 he married Anne of Cleves because he thought an alliance with her country would be useful. However, he found her plain and boring, and for a second time he had a divorce arranged.

He then took a fifth wife, young Catherine Howard, but she rapidly met the same fate as Anne Boleyn. When it was discovered that she had lovers, she was executed in 1542.

Henry's last wife, who was older than the others had been, was Catherine Parr, a kindly widow who nursed the King who now suffered from an ulcerous leg. She also befriended the three children left by his former wives. She made the last three years of his life more tranquil than any of his younger or prettier wives had done.

Henry was a popular king, despite his ruthless executions. He kept order without needing an army. He created a huge navy which was as large as Spain's. His palaces and his court were gorgeous, and his vigorous action against the greedy monks and abbots pleased many people. Whatever his private life may have been like, he did much to make England great in the sixteenth century.

Edward VI 1547–1553

Age 10–16. Son of Henry VIII. Unmarried. Died from consumption.
Buried in Westminster Abbey.

This boy-king reigned under the protection of his uncle, the Protestant Duke of Somerset, who pushed even further than Henry had done the division between the old Catholic faith and the new Church of England. To replace the monastery schools he set up many grammar schools. He introduced the *Book of Common Prayer*, to be used in all church services in place of the Latin Mass. He also had statues of saints broken, and their pictures whitewashed over.

All this caused resentment in some areas and revolts broke out. Kett's Rebellion at Norwich was ruthlessly put down by the Duke of Northumberland, a schemer who then imprisoned (and later executed) Somerset and took over himself.

The country was in a poor state. Prices and rents were high, land once open to all was enclosed for the use of a few. Poor people who trapped or shot the game belonging to a lord were savagely punished.

Throughout these bad years Edward was just a puppet, kept hard at work on his Latin and Greek school-books.

When he became gravely ill with consumption, he and Northumberland rightly feared that Catholicism would return if his half-sister Mary succeeded to the throne. So he signed a document leaving the crown to his cousin Lady Jane Grey, whom Northumberland quickly married to his own son. Within a year Edward was dead.

Mary I 1553–1558

Age 37–42. Daughter of Henry VIII. Married Philip (Spanish).
No children. Buried in Westminster Abbey.

Mary's mother, Catherine of Aragon, had taught her to hold fast to the Catholic religion; and now she found that, because of this, a Protestant usurper – the seventeen-year-old Lady Jane Grey – was being placed by Northumberland on the throne that was hers. So Mary acted swiftly:

Jane had reigned for only nine days when Mary and her supporters (including her Protestant half-sister, Elizabeth) marched into London. The plotter Northumberland was executed and, soon after, poor Jane herself.

Mary then chose a Catholic king to marry, Philip II of Spain, king of her mother's homeland. He was a disastrous choice, for the English feared their country would become part of the Spanish empire. Riots followed, including the Wyatt Rebellion. But Mary did not heed them, and allowed Philip to involve England in his war with France, which resulted in the loss of Calais – the last English possession in Europe. 'The name of Calais will always be engraved on my heart,' said Mary bitterly.

The Queen then began to earn the name by which she is still remembered – Bloody Mary. Protestants were beheaded or burnt alive: three hundred were killed in a mere three years. When Bishops Latimer and Ridley were suffering at the stake in Oxford, Latimer cried out through the flames, 'We shall this day light such a candle in England as shall never be put out.' For generations to come the country would be shaken by religious hostilities.

It is hardly surprising that when Mary died there was more rejoicing than mourning.

Elizabeth I 1558—1603

Age 25–69. Daughter of Henry VIII. Unmarried.
Buried in Westminster Abbey.

England was in a sad state when Elizabeth came to the throne after a lonely and often threatened childhood and youth. She had, in fact, spent much of it imprisoned.

Money was short. There was religious strife. France was thinking of invading England. There were some of her subjects who thought that she, daughter of the beheaded Anne Boleyn, had no right to the crown. Others thought *no* woman could make a good ruler. But Elizabeth, who was both clever and reasonable, turned out to be one of England's greatest monarchs, and earned the title Gloriana.

Although she wanted to avoid wars, events forced them on her. The Huguenots, French Protestants, were being persecuted in Catholic France. In Paris, there had been a terrible massacre of them on St Bartholomew's Day. Spain, also Catholic, was trying to extend her control over more and more countries. Elizabeth sent an army to France to help the Huguenots, and another to free that part of the Netherlands (now called Belgium) which Spain had conquered. She rejected an offer of marriage from the Spanish King, Philip (previously married to her half-sister Mary), and turned down many other suitors too. For none, when king, would have ruled her subjects with the same love and care that she gave them.

Elizabeth had a genius for selecting gifted men to help her, such as William Cecil who was her honest and business-like Lord Treasurer (rather like the Prime Minister of today). Another was Drake. When Spain was building up a dangerously large fleet, the Armada, Drake boldly sailed right into Cadiz harbour and set fire to the lot – 'singeing the King of Spain's beard', he called it. It was he who finally defeated the Armada when it eventually sailed to invade England in 1588.

Drake, Raleigh and others also went on historic voyages of exploration, starting colonies in America, amassing treasure from all round the world, and trading far and wide. The famous East India Company was founded at the end of Elizabeth's reign.

1580

At home meantime, Catholics repeatedly plotted against their Protestant queen. They wanted to supplant her with Mary Queen of Scots, who as grandchild of Henry VII, had the next-best claim to the throne of England. Reluctantly Elizabeth imprisoned her, and then, after nearly twenty years, had her executed in 1587 at Fotheringhay Castle because of her plotting in 1587. The two queens never even met. Elizabeth had no wish to persecute anyone for their religious beliefs, but when these went hand in hand with treason she was forced to act firmly. Puritans also proved troublesome. They were Protestants who wanted to alter the Church of England (to 'purify' it, they said), and to make people dress more plainly and spend less time on amusements.

In spite of all the dangers besetting England, the country flourished as Elizabeth protected it from enemies outside and inside. It was a time when many handsome buildings were built, and costume became rich and elaborate, often encrusted with jewels which the explorers brought home. Shakespeare and many other writers entertained the court with their plays and poetry. Industry prospered. Forests were stripped of timber to build great ships. Iron was mined to make cannons, and coal to smelt the iron and to heat homes in place of wood. London now began to get smoky with Newcastle coal. Even more men, however, were employed in brewing beer than in mining coal.

It was the rich lords and merchants who provided the money to start all these new enterprises – and they took the profits. How wealthy they became can be seen from their many handsome houses which still remain and can be visited today – houses such as Montacute (Somerset), Melford Hall (Suffolk) and Hardwick Hall (Derbyshire).

The Queen loved flattery and she flirted with many suitors – Robert Dudley, Earl of Leicester, and later the young and treacherous Earl of Essex were her two favourites. But she never married, for whatever her personal feelings may have been, there was no man to whom she was prepared to entrust the throne.

When she died, still single, at Richmond Palace, a rider sped swiftly to Scotland to inform her rightful successor, James VI of Scotland, the son of Mary Queen of Scots, that he was now King of England too.

Elizabeth, last of the Tudors, had a brilliant mind, spoke many languages, excelled at dancing and archery, and even to the end of her life had a most royal and splendid appearance. She could be witty, melancholy or furiously angry in turn. In marked contrast to so many rulers, she did not side with her barons or any upstart favourites but loved the common people and shared the perils that faced them (even going to the army at Tilbury, in Essex, when the Spanish invasion was expected).

In the last speech to her people before her death she said, 'Though you have had, and may have, many Princes more mighty and wise, yet you never had or shall have any that will be more careful or loving.'

James I 1603–1625

Age 37–59. Great-great-grandson of Henry VII.
Married Anne (Danish). Seven children.
Buried in Westminster Abbey.

Now Scotland provided England with a new line of kings, the Stuarts. They were to bring disaster to the nation for, coming from Scotland where royal power had not been curbed by Parliament, they had no understanding of the more democratic ways that had developed in England.

James, son of Mary Queen of Scots, had had a terrible childhood. His father, Lord Darnley, had been murdered a few months after his birth and, from the time he was a baby, his mother had languished as a prisoner in England. He was surrounded by plotters, spies, rebels, assassins, and war-makers, and grew up in the care of an exceedingly harsh guardian. Twice he was kidnapped and then released.

When he was a year old he became King of Scotland after his mother had been forced to abdicate. Once he was old enough to rule the country and its turbulent lords, he did so wisely.

When Elizabeth died, the two countries which had so long been hostile were brought together under one sovereign and given a name devised by James himself, Great Britain. Their flags – the red-on-white cross of St George and the white-on-blue cross of St Andrew – were combined in a design that was the beginning of the Union Jack.

James believed that kings had a God-given right to rule, and he was not prepared to let Parliament make laws against his own wishes. Parliament retaliated by refusing to raise money through taxation to pay all the heavy expenses of his courtiers. Just how luxuriously they lived can be seen from their homes, places like Audley End in Essex, and Hatfield House in Hertfordshire, both of which can still be visited today.

Discontent took an explosive turn when, in 1605, Guy Fawkes and some other Catholic conspirators tried to assassinate the King. Their plan was to blow up Parliament when he went there on November 5th, but they were discovered lurking in the cellars just in time. The plot made the Catholics even more unpopular than before.

1620

The Puritans too were resented just as much because they wanted to cut out all church ceremonials and end the power of the bishops. In 1620 some of them decided to try and start a new and 'purer' community of their own in America, and they set sail from Plymouth in the *Mayflower*, earning themselves an historic nickname, the Pilgrim Fathers.

James was a learned man who encouraged many worthy scholars. It was he who ordered the first really good English translation of the Bible to be made in 1611 – the Authorized Version. Since then about a hundred million copies of this version have been printed.

But James was also weak. For example, in 1618 he gave in to Spanish pressure to execute that country's age-old foe, the courageous Raleigh.

Despite all Elizabeth's successes, Spain and England were still at war when James came to the throne, but he soon made a peace treaty, and he even tried to marry his son Charles to a Spanish princess. In spite of these efforts he later found himself drawn into a fresh war with Spain – the Thirty Years War – on behalf of his son-in-law, whose Protestant kingdom of Bohemia, now Czechoslovakia, had been attacked by Catholic Spain. A few years later he died.

James's harsh and loveless childhood had left him with a distrustful mind and permanently downcast eyes and mouth. A rather untidy man with a strong Scots accent, he disliked ceremony and was never popular. In spite of all this his Danish wife loved him dearly. She, by contrast, was beautiful and gay. While James amused himself with his zoo in the Tower of London or on the racetrack which he built at Newmarket, she planned lavish entertainments at court and commissioned the famous architect Inigo Jones to build such delightful mansions as Queen's House at Greenwich and the Banqueting House in Whitehall.

Charles I 1625–1649

Age 25–49. Son of James I. Married Henrietta Maria (French).
Nine children. Executed. Buried at Windsor.

Charles, who had been ill with polio as a child, nevertheless grew up to have a strong and courageous character despite his short height, his shyness and his lifelong stammer. Unfortunately he was also stubborn, tactless, and much given to breaking promises. He married a gay French wife who was Catholic and unpopular. Then he rapidly quarrelled with Parliament because, like his father, he refused to give way on any point and asserted that he had a divine right to rule, to impose taxes and to imprison anyone who obstructed him.

Because he then declined to summon Parliament at all, he had to find other ways to raise money on his own. One of his least popular methods was to demand 'ship money' from every town to pay for the navy.

1640

Meantime, the war with Spain dragged on. Charles allowed some Catholic rituals to creep back into the Church of England, and the causes of discontent steadily mounted. When in 1642 Charles forced his way into the House of Commons in an attempt to arrest five MPs who had refused him loans, civil war broke out.

For four years the struggle tore the nation apart. The Parliament army (the Roundheads) had the support of many townspeople, the rich ports, and some nobles; while the Royalists (Cavaliers) were supported by the nobles, who sold their gold plate to help, and by the peasants.

Of many battles, the most important was in 1645 when Cromwell led the Roundheads to victory at Naseby (Leicestershire). By midday there was 'not a horse or man of the King's army to be seen except the prisoners'. Although outnumbered two-to-one, the Cavaliers had fought gallantly, with Charles himself as their brave commander – but in vain.

Charles tried to take refuge in Scotland but was handed back to England and imprisoned at Hampton Court. He escaped to the Isle of Wight and from there encouraged a fresh outbreak of fighting – again, unsuccessfully. He was doomed. No less than 135 judges were assembled to try him for being a 'tyrant, traitor and murderer'. By a majority of only one vote, the judges condemned him to death.

He was publicly beheaded outside his banqueting house in Whitehall in the snow. Stunned crowds saw the executioner hold his severed head aloft. One voice called out, 'Behold the head of a traitor!' But from thousands present there came, said one observer, 'such a groan as I never heard before and desire I may never hear again'. Charles's last word was, 'Remember . . .' and to this day he *is* remembered by many as Charles the Martyr.

Like other disastrous kings Charles I nevertheless brought about many good things we enjoy today. Much of the money he extracted from his complaining subjects went on fine buildings, which he then filled with paintings by geniuses like Van Dyck and Rubens. He was a good husband and father, a very good rider and shot, wrote well and took his responsibilities seriously. He deserved a better fate, even though his execution was essential to end despotism.

The Commonwealth 1649–1660

During the Civil War, Oliver Cromwell had been a brilliant commander, and his New Model Army (nicknamed the Ironsides) won many a victory. After King Charles's execution he became Lord Protector of what was now known as the Commonwealth, for Britain was no longer a kingdom.

As the years passed, however, the Commonwealth system turned out to have disadvantages. Although it produced a number of good things, like the opening of more schools, and better care for the poor, people began to resent being controlled by an army. They also hated the puritanical laws – for instance, travel on a Sunday was forbidden; there were severe punishments for swearing; horseracing was banned; many public houses were closed down; and statues and other ornaments in churches were smashed. There were many Puritan sects now with differing views: some, for instance, were vigorously opposed to the army, and to priests of any kind. As a result, the Puritans began to disagree among themselves, and there was a fear that more civil war might result.

When Cromwell died he was buried with much pomp in Westminster Abbey (later he was dug up) and his son Richard took his place. But Tumbledown Dick as they called him was a poor ruler, endless disagreements broke out, and it was not long before all parties agreed to invite the Stuarts back to the throne in the person of Charles II.

Charles II 1660–1685

Age 30–55. Son of Charles I. Married Catherine (Portuguese). No children. Buried in Westminster Abbey.

The Merry Monarch they called him because of his fondness for witty conversation, fine clothes and girl-friends such as Nell Gwynn, the orange-seller. But although he was none too keen on hard work or listening to sermons, there was a serious side to him too; not surprisingly, for the first half of his life had been full of danger and tragedy.

When only twelve, he had fought alongside his father in the Civil War, and was then forced to flee to France. When one chilly morning his chaplain came with news and began by addressing him as 'Your Majesty . . .', he knew without further words what the news was, and burst into tears. He returned to Scotland to lead an army south against the Cromwellians. Battle was joined at Worcester. After three hours, when all the Royalist ammunition was gone, his men still fought on with musket butts and pikes until half of them were dead and the city's streets filled with corpses. Charles escaped and, disguised as a peasant with his hair cropped short, made for the coast. At Boscobel (Shropshire) he had to hide in an oak while the Roundheads searched for him below. After more narrow escapes and much difficulty in getting a ship, he at last sailed to France again.

Secretly Charles wanted to be Catholic, but he knew there would be little support for him in England or Scotland if he let this be known, so he outwardly adopted Protestant ways. After Cromwell died Charles was invited to return. Fountains were filled with wine and the streets were strewn with flowers.

But there were wars with the Dutch now (caused by disputes over fishing and trading rights), followed by the Great Plague of 1665 and the Great Fire of 1666. The King himself helped to save many citizens' goods in this terrible four-day fire. Then came an appalling winter when even the Thames froze. In 1667 the Dutch sailed up the Medway and towed off or burned the English fleet's finest ships from Chatham.

There was continued wrangling over religion too. Both the Catholics and the Nonconformists (the extreme Protestant groups) were prevented by law from becoming MPs or army officers, and were accused of plotting against the King. Two political parties began to take shape – the Tories, who supported the King, and the Whigs, who wanted more power for Parliament. This was a time of craftiness in politics. MPs accepted bribes to vote this way or that; Charles signed secret agreements (for instance, with France) of which Parliament knew nothing, in order to obtain funds from abroad; and, like his father, he sometimes stopped Parliament from even meeting.

Nevertheless, in his reign there were many noble achievements. Some great men lived then too, such as the architect Christopher Wren (who designed St Paul's and many other churches when London was rebuilt after the Great Fire), the poet Milton, Purcell the composer, the diarist Samuel Pepys and Isaac Newton the scientist.

One wintry night the King fell ill. In his bedroom his spaniels dozed by the coal fire and his several clocks chimed away the last hours of his life. 'Let not poor Nelly starve,' he said, and then he died, to be truly mourned by his people, popular in spite of all his faults.

James II 1685–1688

Age 52–55. Son of Charles I. Married Anne (English) then Mary (Italian).
Fifteen children. Buried in Paris.

As Charles II had no children, his Catholic brother James succeeded him.

Some anti-Catholics then tried to rebel and to replace him with the Duke of Monmouth, the illegitimate son of Charles II, but this revolt was crushed at the night battle of Sedgemoor (Somerset) in 1685. Hundreds of rebels were then tried by 'Hanging Judge Jeffreys' and transported, hanged or flogged. Monmouth was executed.

James now began to persecute all Protestants and to give important posts to Catholics. This was intolerable to many people, and it seemed like the last straw when James became the father of a son who did not, like previous male babies, die in infancy. For this meant that there was now an heir to the throne who would also be Catholic.

Thoughts turned to James's daughter Mary, who was Protestant and married to a Dutch Protestant prince,  William of Orange. By invitation of seven leading bishops and others, William agreed to land in Devon with an army to assert his wife's claim to the throne.

James was deposed without any trouble, for the English army refused to support him against William. The invasion, known as the Glorious Revolution, had happened without so much as a drop of blood being shed. Panic-stricken, James fled to France where he eventually died.

William III and Mary II
1689–1702, 1689–1694

Ages 39–52, 27–32, Mary was daughter of James II.
Married William (Dutch). No children. Mary died 1694, William 1702.
Both buried in Westminster Abbey.

The two new monarchs had been welcomed on condition that they agreed to a Bill of Rights which said that no king or queen could ignore the laws of the land, keep an army going when there was no war on, or prevent Parliament meeting regularly. This made it plain that kings do not have a God-given right to rule, but depend upon the will of Parliament.

The Dutchman William, hunchbacked and rather grouchy, ruled fairly and persecuted no one for religious reasons. By her own choice, Mary left all the power in his hands. He had to deal with trouble in Scotland, where James had supporters. He established the Bank of England, and encouraged the construction of fine houses, furniture and gardens.

Much of his reign was spent at war with France, mainly because of French threats to Holland, his own country. James continually plotted against William. His followers became known as Jacobites (Jacobus is Latin for James).

Mary died from smallpox and William was later killed when his horse stumbled on a molehill. 'Here's to the little gentleman in black velvet,' joked the delighted Jacobites.

Anne 1702–1714

Age 37–49   Daughter of James II. Married George (Danish).
Seventeen children. Buried in Westminster Abbey.

Anne was a very ordinary woman, not well educated, who spent most of her time and energy giving birth to babies, every one of which soon died. Yet her short reign was full of brilliance because it happened to be a time when famous men flourished. Writers like Swift and Pope lived then, for instance, and so did the military genius, the Duke of Marlborough (ancestor of Winston Churchill). Marlborough won victory after victory in battles against France, making England the leader of the world and at last halting the spread of French power in Europe. The most famous of his battles are Blenheim, Ramillies, Oudenarde and Malplaquet – his magnificent palace in Oxfordshire is named after the first of these battles.

Marlborough's witty and clever wife Sarah was a great favourite of the Queen, until they quarrelled over politics in 1711 and the Queen cast her off: the Marlboroughs wanted to see some Whigs in the Government, but Anne wanted only Tories.

At last, in 1713, hostilities came to an end. The peace treaty, signed at Utrecht in 1713, was an important one for Britain because it gave her possession of Gibraltar, colonies in America and other territory, and control of the profitable (though evil) slave trade from Africa to America.

The reign of 'good Queen Anne' was notable for two other things. England and Scotland were at last made one country by the Act of Union (1707). And in 1704 the Queen provided a fund to help the clergy (some of whom were now very poor): this was called Queen Anne's Bounty.

Poor Anne had a dreary life – usually in pain from gout, or mourning her dead children. Her conscience continually pricked her, for she realized that the throne really belonged to her younger half-brother, who had been dispossessed when William and Mary invaded, and who was now an exile in France. She consoled herself by playing cards and drinking tea (a new fashion). When she died, her doctor said, 'Sleep was never more welcome to a weary traveller than death was to her.'

1714   1720

George I 1714–1727

Age 54–67. Great-grandson of James I. Married Sophia (German).
Two children. Buried in Hanover (Germany).

Anne being childless despite so many births, a new family of monarchs now took over the throne – the Hanoverians, from north Germany. In 1701 Parliament had passed a law (the Act of Settlement) under which a distant cousin of the Queen was to become king after her. He was the Elector (or ruler) of Hanover who, being Protestant, was preferred to Anne's Catholic half-brother, nicknamed the Old Pretender.

George could hardly speak English and spent most of the time in his beloved Hanover. So, unlike earlier kings, he left power in the hands of the Whig ministers whom he selected – a big change that meant from now on parliaments were going to be more powerful than kings.

The Whigs governed the country under a Norfolk squire, Sir Robert Walpole, the first real Prime Minister of Britain and the first to live at 10 Downing Street. When Walpole came to power, he ran the country like a tough businessman, aiming for prosperity and low taxes.

The British people had at first accepted their German king: 'not a mouse stirred against him'. But many of the discontented Tories, who wanted to get rid of both Walpole and King George, soon plotted with the Jacobites to bring back the Old Pretender, a Stuart. However, their rebellion in 1715 was a complete flop.

George, who was plump, pop-eyed and pigheaded, was more interested in horses than in either politics or court ceremonials, and he even wanted to grow turnips in the royal parks. He quarrelled with his wife, imprisoning her for life in a German castle, and with his son. But at least he appreciated good music and gave the composer Handel employment in Britain.

George II 1727–1760

Age 44–77. Son of George I. Married Caroline (German). Eight children. Buried in Westminster Abbey.

This George too was first and foremost a German ruler, but he understood English somewhat better than his father had. Father and son had hated one another, so when George II came to the throne he dismissed George I's adviser Walpole – only to find that he could not manage without this clever politician. His flirtatious but intelligent wife Caroline persuaded him to make Walpole Prime Minister once more.

It was Walpole who introduced the first Cabinet, a group of ministers to govern the country, drawn only from the dominant political party – in this case the Whigs. The Cabinet was to be answerable to Parliament, with Parliament answerable to the electors. But at that time, only men who owned land had a vote, so Britain was still far from being truly democratic.

The year 1739 saw the outbreak of more wars, which were to last beyond the end of the century. Though Walpole encouraged peace, the King and others longed for military adventures. First came wars with Spain. The real reason was to do with trading rivalries, but quite different incidents triggered off the War of Jenkins' Ear. A sea captain trading with Spanish colonies had, he said, had his ear slashed off by Spanish coastguards – he had it on show in a bottle. When war was declared to avenge him, the people thronged the streets, cheering. Walpole said, 'They are ringing the bells now but soon they will be wringing their hands.' They sang a new tune, *Rule Britannia*, but Walpole was right about the defeats that were to come when the wars extended and Britain found herself unsuccessfully fighting Hanoverian causes against France.

Meantime, the Jacobites were again trying to restore the Stuarts to the throne. The Old Pretender had died, but in 1745 there was a rebellion led by his son, the Young Pretender – Bonnie Prince Charlie. He landed in Scotland, marched into England as far as Derby, but had to retreat and was finally defeated at the battle of Culloden.

1740

The British suffered so many defeats in their French wars that the Government became too unpopular to continue. In addition, Walpole had attempted to put an unpopular tax on wine and tobacco because so much of this was smuggled in without paying any duty at the ports. Even though he had made the country so prosperous, Walpole had had to resign in 1742 (after twenty-one years of power) and his place had been taken by another Whig, the aggressive William Pitt. From 1757 onwards Britain won many sea victories, and made conquests in Canada and India, where Wolfe and Clive became famous for their exploits.

George, who had not been on speaking terms with his father, had an even worse relationship with his eldest son Frederick, whom he called 'the greatest ass, the greatest liar and the greatest beast in the whole world', although Frederick was only rather foolish – and much more popular than the King. 'His popularity makes me vomit,' said his jealous father. His son retaliated, 'The King is an obstinate, miserly martinet,' and that was what a lot of people felt at his court and in the country as a whole. When attempts were made to stop so much heavy drinking (cheap gin caused a lot of drunkenness, and made the poor even poorer), crowds thumped his coach as he went by, yelling, 'No gin, no King!' But he became more popular after the battle of Dettingen (1743), where he himself led the army crying, 'Fire and behave brave! The French will run.' (Which they did.) He was the last British king to lead an army himself. Brave he may have been, but he was also mean and rather ridiculous.

George III 1760–1820

Age 22–81. Grandson of George II. Married Charlotte (German). Fifteen children. Buried at Windsor.

George II's son Frederick having already died, it was his grandson who now became king. He was a good-looking, amiable and deeply religious young man, who was the first monarch since Queen Anne to speak good English and to put British interests well before those of Hanover. He believed, too, that the king should have an effective say in running the country, and that his Whig ministers must work closely with him. There were many changes among his ministers until he got one, Lord North, with whom he could work smoothly.

George III's reign is often remembered, rather unfairly, for just one big event which was considered a national disaster at the time – the American War of Independence. America was populated by British settlers who had to obey many laws laid down in London, and pay some taxes to Britain. Although they numbered one-fifth of the King's subjects, they were not represented in Parliament. The taxes got heavier and heavier until the settlers were angered into revolting. The incident that started it all was the Boston Tea Party. In 1773, some settlers boarded a ship waiting in Boston harbour to unload some tea (on which new taxes would have to be paid) and threw the lot overboard. Later they tarred and feathered one of the Customs men whose job it was to collect the taxes. Next year, the settlers started their own parliament (called Congress) and demanded that the King should end their grievances. Instead, he sent soldiers to keep them in order. The settlers responded by starting their own army, commanded by George Washington, and in 1775 the war started. It dragged on for six years before Britain gave up and the Americans became an independent nation. The King was so stricken by this that he almost abdicated.

Gradually the King began to give his ministers more freedom of action. In 1783 he accepted William Pitt the Younger (twenty-four-year-old son of the Pitt who had succeeded Walpole) who now became the first Tory Prime Minister, and the youngest Prime Minister in history. He stayed in power for more than twenty years, and was in control throughout most of the wars fought to subdue Napoleon (1793–1815).

It was during the Napoleonic Wars that Nelson and Wellington respectively won their great victories at Trafalgar and Waterloo.

There were important events at home, too, such as the Act of Union (1801) which brought Ireland, like Scotland, into one kingdom with England; and a law to abolish slave-trading (1807), although slavery itself still continued.

The King was known as Farmer George because of his interest in the many improved ways of farming which were coming in during his reign. 'Many a time,' wrote one man who had spent his boyhood at Windsor, 'had he bidden us good morning when we were hunting for mushrooms in the early dew and he was returning from his dairy to his 8 o'clock breakfast.' He often walked, unattended and plainly dressed, in the local streets where he chatted with people. When at home, he lived a quiet life, riding or hunting, taking meals alone with his family (his favourite dish was mutton with turnips), listening to music while the Queen sewed, playing cards or chess, drinking tea and going to bed early. Small balls of a few dozen people were his usual birthday celebration; sea-bathing at Weymouth in Dorset his favourite holiday. His servants were devoted to him – and so were his subjects.

He was also interested in the theatre and music: he played several instruments himself, and once listened to Mozart play at the age of eight. He loved gardens: the Botanical Gardens at Kew were created by him. His interest in the boys at Eton College was so great that he spent a lot of time there and, to this day, they still celebrate his birthday on 4 June. In order to watch the stars, he built himself an observatory; and gave the scientist Herschel the money to build the biggest telescope in the world, which led to Herschel's revolutionary discoveries about the universe. Some of the many scientific instruments the King collected can still be seen in London's Science Museum; and all the merino sheep in Australia owe their existence to a new breed which George developed. His collection of rare books became the beginning of the famous British Museum library; and it was he who founded the Royal Academy. And all this tremendous list of achievements is to the credit of someone who, as a boy, had been thought lazy and backward, and as an old man was to be dismissed as crazy.

In 1811 he became ill with a rare disease called porphyria which affected his mind and sometimes made him blind too. His eldest son had to rule in his place as Prince Regent. The forty-nine-year-old Prince had always been treated as a child by his father, and there had been endless quarrels between them.

When the Prince was a boy, he had been kept at his studies twelve hours a day. He was allowed only four hours' play a week. As soon as he grew up, the Prince got into scrapes: his father had to pay his debts, there were public scandals about an actress and another man's wife whom the Prince took as girl-friends, he over-ate and frequently got drunk, he spent money wildly on furniture, clothes and jewellery – and he sided with his father's political enemies.

Worse was to come. In 1784 he secretly went through a marriage ceremony with a Catholic widow, Mrs Fitzherbert. This was despite the fact that in 1772 the King had got Parliament to pass a Royal Marriage Act under which members of the royal family had (and still have) to get the monarch's consent before marrying. And as no one married to a Catholic was allowed to succeed to the throne (that had been laid down in an Act of 1701 when Anne became Queen), King George would not accept Mrs Fitzherbert. In spite of this, the Prince found a disreputable priest (in prison for debt) whom he bribed to perform the ceremony.

By 1794, however, the Prince began to regret his secret marriage, for now he wanted to marry a rich German princess. So he readily admitted the wedding had not been a legal one, took the princess as his wife – and then began to regret that too, for she proved a sore trial to him.

Perhaps it is not too surprising that on one occasion the ailing King – red-eyed and foaming at the mouth – tried to smash his son's head against a wall. But the doctors said the King was mad and had him shut up in Kew Palace, tied to his bed or a chair whenever he seemed violent.

Later he seemed to recover for a while, but for the last ten years of his life he was confined in Windsor Castle – blind, with a straggling beard, wearing only a dressing-gown, always in pain and often with his mind wandering.

When he died, he was buried at his much-loved Windsor and not in Westminster Abbey, and it is there that all monarchs since have their tombs.

1800

The eighteenth century as a whole was remarkable for its splendours, and its miseries – many of which were most notable in George III's long reign, during which the country's population doubled.

There were dozens of famous writers, such as Dr Johnson, Jane Austen, Walter Scott, Byron, Horace Walpole, Wordsworth, Shelley and Keats. Some of the most outstanding painters lived then too, including Gainsborough, Romney, Hogarth and Reynolds.

Big changes took place in the appearance of England. Canals were built, and the first smooth-surfaced roads constructed. The style of architecture changed completely, with houses and churches now being designed in a manner that was based on Greek or Roman styles, with stately columns and more restrained decoration. The Adam brothers were the most famous architects of this style, Chippendale, Hepplewhite and Sheraton designed furniture in keeping with such buildings, and Wedgwood used similar classical ideas in his china. The King built himself a new home, Buckingham House (later enlarged into Buckingham Palace), and a new state coach (still used whenever the monarch opens Parliament). No wonder this period was called the 'golden age' of English design.

These things, however, were only for the wealthy, and it was still only the wealthy who had a say in how the country should be run. George realized that the House of Commons had greatly extended its power during this century, and he believed it was time the Crown should again have a more effective say in things – though he had no aim to be a despot, like the Stuart kings. He wanted to see a balance of power between Crown and Parliament, freedom of speech, and just law-courts.

All this was sound; but still left the majority of ordinary people without any way of voicing their grievances in Parliament. As a consequence, London was often disturbed by angry and violent mobs demonstrating in the streets and attacking politicians' houses and coaches (there was no police force to stop them). Newspaper comments and cartoons were often abusive and defamatory (there were no libel laws to restrain them).

Sometimes riots occurred in which people were killed: the worst were the week-long Gordon Riots of 1780, triggered off by a Protestant–Catholic dispute started by Lord George Gordon. Some people feared, when the French Revolution broke out in 1789, that Britain would follow suit.

What were the grievances that caused all this upset? The poor lived in a state of overcrowded squalor and hunger. Brutality was normal: for minor offences, people were flung into the harshest of prisons running with damp and filth, or hanged while crowds watched. These were the people who had no votes, and it was small consolation that they were also exempt from taxes and from military service. Governments showed no interest in their welfare, but were concerned with two things only – keeping law and order, and controlling relationships with foreign countries.

The next century would see a change.

George IV 1820–1830

Age 58–67. Son of George III.
Married Mrs Fitzherbert (English), then Caroline (German). One child.
Buried at Windsor.

As Prince Regent with his own fashionable court, George had become known as 'the first gentleman of Europe'. He dressed his fat figure in elegant clothes and furnished Carlton House in the latest mode (no expense spared!) which was to become known as the Regency style. He spent lavishly on new buildings, like the fanciful Indian-looking pavilion at Brighton, where he made seaside excursions popular for the first time; on Nash's designs for Regent Street and Regent's Park; on portraits by Lawrence; and other beautiful luxuries. His extravagance at a time when so many people lived in dire poverty was shocking. So was his treatment of his wife, Princess Caroline, silly and vulgar though she was: he was drunk at their wedding, he later tried to divorce her, and he prevented her from joining in his spectacular coronation. She retaliated by making scenes and travelling in Europe with an Italian lover.

Yet George had some good qualities too. He loved reading – he was a great admirer of Jane Austen and Walter Scott – he persuaded the Government to buy the paintings needed to start the National Gallery, and he was exceptionally intelligent and witty too. He meddled foolishly in politics, and was much better at planning building projects than at affairs of state. He opposed every kind of reform, including even the Catholic Emancipation Act (1829) which allowed Catholics to become MPs for the first time. His people both loved him for his kindly nature and hated his follies.

When he died, he was still wearing a miniature of Mrs Fitzherbert.

William IV 1830–1837

Age 65–71. Son of George III. Married Adelaide (German). No children. Buried at Windsor.

George IV's only daughter having died young, he was succeeded by one of his brothers, William, Duke of Clarence, known as Sailor George because of his years as a naval officer. Of all the royal dukes, bluff William was the most steady, thrifty and reliable – quite unlike George. He hated pomp and lavish display. It was in his reign that the great Reform Act (1832) was passed, in spite of vigorous opposition from the House of Lords. This Act gave the vote to every man owning a little property, about one man in every six, and in the next hundred years it was gradually extended to all men and women, regardless of their means.

Other reforms in William's reign included the abolition of slavery, provision for the poor, the organizing of the first police force, and better local government. In other countries at this time, reforms were being secured by revolutions and the overthrow of monarchies, but the good-natured and sensible William (whom his brothers had nicknamed Silly Billy!) survived, and so Britain remained a kingdom.

1830   1837   1840

Victoria 1837–1901

Age 18–81. Grand-daughter of George III. Married Albert (German). Nine children. Buried at Windsor (Frogmore Mausoleum).

William IV had no children, and since his younger brother, the Duke of Kent, was dead, the throne now went to his niece Victoria, who was scarcely more than a child. Her power-loving German mother thought that she would do the ruling in Victoria's name, but from the very first day Victoria made it plain who was Queen.

Within three years, Victoria married her handsome German cousin Albert, whom she adored. Nevertheless, she would not let him be king, although he was in due course given the title of Prince Consort. Behind the scenes, however, she took his advice on how to rule. He was a serious, careful man and between the two of them the royal court became very respectable and the royal family was held up as an example of good behaviour – quite unlike the Hanoverian and Stuart monarchies. Albert had several inspired ideas: one was the Great Exhibition of 1851, held in the Crystal Palace specially built for it in Hyde Park, at which every imaginable product of British industry and art was put on display; and another was the tradition of Christmas trees.

In 1861, Prince Albert became very ill with typhoid, a deadly fever due to bad drains which killed many people at that time. Suffering though he was, he got up from his bed because there was a crisis between America and Britain – but for his intervention, there might have been war. This was his last important act: he died soon afterwards.

The Queen grieved bitterly, and for the rest of her life always wore black. For years she would not go out. She spent a lot of time in the house at Balmoral in Scotland which she and Albert had bought together, and later at Osborne House on the Isle of Wight. Often she preferred the company of an old Scottish servant, John Brown, to any of the lords or ladies of her court.

Nevertheless, she worked exceedingly hard behind the scenes and insisted that her ministers consult her about everything that was going on. Times had changed, and governments now were answerable to the

House of Commons, not the monarch: without the approval of a majority of MPs, ministers would soon lose office. Nevertheless, Victoria had such a strong personality and such a good grasp of politics, that she had a lot of say in what went on.

And much was going on during her long reign. At last, now that more ordinary people had a vote, Parliament was paying attention to the needs of even the poorest sections of the public. Because factories, equipped with the new high-speed machinery, had taken over many kinds of work, like weaving, formerly done by hand in the villages, there had been a vast change in living conditions. The coming of the railways too, had changed Britain dramatically. The benefits of cheap, mass-produced clothing, and quick transportation of goods and people, were offset by the fact that the hand craftsmen had lost their livelihood, or had been forced to move into the cities where the factories provided jobs. Cheaply built houses were crammed together, without proper water supplies or drains, and overcrowded slums and disease were the result. The factory owners paid so little that families went hungry, so the mothers and children worked too, often for very long hours in dirty and dangerous conditions.

During Victoria's reign, these problems were tackled by a series of laws which, one by one, made it illegal for women and children to work underground in coal-mines; limited working hours to ten a day; provided free schooling for children; improved the standards of housing, and provided drains; and at last made it legal for workers to band together in trade unions in order to get fair wages and decent working conditions. Although Victoria and Albert supported these reforms, demonstrators against the State tried to assassinate her on seven different occasions.

Many famous Prime Ministers were responsible for these Acts, among them two who became close friends of the Queen – Melbourne (Whig) and Disraeli (Tory). She disliked Palmerston (Tory) and Gladstone (Liberal). The Liberals were a new political party which stood for giving the vote and better living conditions to more of the ordinary people, with less power for the House of Lords; and for allowing Ireland to have its

1860

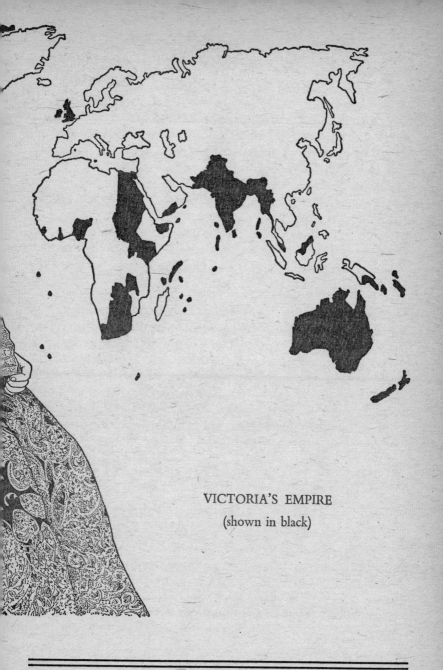

VICTORIA'S EMPIRE

(shown in black)

1880

own government. The Conservatives (as the Tories now began to be called) were more interested in spreading the British Empire over even more parts of the world.

Victoria was more than a Queen – she became Empress of India too. For now Britain's possessions overseas were multiplying fast (sometimes by agreement, sometimes as a result of military conquest) until the British Empire covered a large part of the world: New Zealand, Canada, Australia, Burma, Egypt, South Africa and, of course, India were all dominated by Britain. Wars had to be fought in Egypt, India (to suppress a mutiny), and South Africa (against the Boers – Dutch settlers). On the other hand, except for the Crimean War of 1853–6 (to protect Turkey from Russian invasion), there was peace between Britain and European countries – one reason was that the Queen's many children were gradually married into the ruling families of countries such as Germany, Denmark and Russia.

Her eldest son Edward remained Prince of Wales until he was sixty, idling his time away with pursuits of which his mother disapproved. But she would not contemplate the idea of abdicating the throne so that he could take over, and she would not even let him read her official letters. At last she died, at the age of eighty-one. The entire nation was shocked: she had reigned so long that all but the very oldest people could remember no other monarch but her. It seemed inconceivable that there could be any change. But with Edward on the throne at last, a lot of things were to be very, very different from then on.

What was life like in Victorian times? That greatly depended on how well off you were.

A middle-class family might live in a large house with a formal garden, have a lot of servants and even a carriage and horses. Their rooms tended to be crowded with heavily carved furniture, a mass of ornaments and lots of elaborate brass and silver to be polished every week. Dusting was a major chore because of the sooty air created by coal fires, which harmed health as well; and piped hot water was still a luxury. Clothes, too, were to cause the servants still more work on washday (remember, there were no detergents, electric irons and washing-machines – no vacuum cleaners either, until the end of the century). Lighting was mostly by gas.

The Victorians liked their public buildings, too, to be showy, which is why we still have so many stations, hotels, libraries, swimming baths, museums and even prisons designed like grand castles or palaces. Even funerals were ornate in a gloomy way.

By contrast, many workers lived in poky, damp and dark little houses, smelly from lack of drains and lavatories, dirty for lack of piped water. It was not uncommon for one family to have a dozen children crammed into one room, but usually many of these died from the diseases that spread in such appalling conditions, and from not having enough food, medical care or exercise. No holidays or toys, of course, little schooling and few books. Many went barefoot, even in winter and even in streets where rats prowled among the garbage in the gutters. People in these conditions were, however, better off than those who, unable to get a job, were sent to one of the detested workhouses, little better than prisons. Only gradually during Victoria's reign were such things changed for the better.

While the poor were glad to get even thin broth doled out by charity-workers, the leisurely rich over-ate: at one meal, they might eat turtle soup, salmon, beef, pheasant, plum-pudding and much more. Their leisure was mostly spent at home – often reading aloud the latest book by Dickens or poem by Tennyson, making music, painting neat little pictures or embroidering fussy little mats and purses, perhaps playing croquet on the lawn. Girls had few opportunities outside this narrow life, unless they went to work as governesses. And on Sunday even these occupations might be forbidden: church-going and Bible-reading could fill the entire day.

It was not only the poor whose way of life was unsatisfying and who were beginning to question whether Victoria's reign was really as 'happy and glorious' as it was made out to be.

Edward VII 1901–1910

Age 60–69. Son of Victoria. Married Alexandra (Danish).
Six children. Buried at Windsor.

At an age when many men are about to retire from work, Edward at last got the job of being king. Everyone thought he would be a disaster – his parents had considered him a fool and he had spent all his life so far as a dandy and playboy, flirting, gambling, over-eating, smoking heavily, staying at the luxurious country houses of rich businessmen to shoot pheasants, racing his yacht and his horses, and so on. But there was another side to him. His warmth and kindness had brought him friends among all kinds of politicians and others (even foreign revolutionaries), so that he had become very well informed about world affairs. He was not, however, much interested in the big changes made by the Liberals during his reign – the first old-age pensions, the start of National Insurance (which meant that workers got some payments when they were ill and unable to earn), free secondary education for all children, and the beginnings of strong trade unions.

Where he played a really important part was in foreign affairs. He visited other countries and helped to create firm alliances, particularly with France, and earned himself the nickname Edward the Peacemaker. But he disliked his nephew, the Kaiser of Germany, and there was growing hostility between Britain and Germany, each of them strengthening their navies in readiness for a possible war.

Edward died suddenly in the middle of a political crisis, which was left to his son to deal with.

George V 1910–1936

Age 45–70. Son of Edward VII. Married Mary (German). Six children.
Buried at Windsor.

George had had a happy childhood, and had become a popular naval
officer for many years, despite a peppery temper and loud voice. During
his father's short reign he helped him with official papers, and began to be
deeply interested in the people's welfare. Already he had begun to
develop a serious interest in public affairs which would be invaluable to
the country in the difficult years that lay ahead.

At the very moment when he came to the throne, Parliament was in an
uproar because the House of Lords had turned down an important
Liberal budget increasing taxes to provide old-age pensions and a better
navy. The Liberals therefore asked the new King to create a lot of fresh
peers certain to vote for the budget, in order to get it through.
Reluctantly the King agreed and this in itself was enough to make the
Lords pass it.

As a result of this crisis, steps were then taken to ensure that nothing like
it could occur again. By the Parliament Act of 1911, the power of the
House of Lords was reduced so that it could only delay Bills for three
years (now one year) and not turn them down completely.

But within a few years, these matters were forgotten in a greater crisis –
war. The King had himself tried to make it clear to his cousin, the
Kaiser of Germany, that Britain would certainly fight if France or Russia
were attacked. In spite of this, Germany declared war on these two
countries (some of whose territories she wanted to annex) and so
Britain came to their aid.

During the war years, the King and Queen regularly mixed with the
people, visiting the Army and Navy, hospitals, and factories. This was
something no monarch had done for two centuries or more.

Even when the war was over, the King and the country were still beset
with problems. There were years of religious conflict in Ireland which
continued, despite George's attempts to get the antagonists to discuss
matters peaceably, until in 1920 it was agreed by Lloyd George (the

1920

Liberal Prime Minister) that Ireland should be divided in two. The northern (mainly Protestant) part remained within Great Britain, and the southern (Catholic) part became an independent country, Eire, within the British Empire.

In England, there was a great deal of unrest and strikes, etc., and in 1924 for the first time the Socialists (the Labour Party) gained power, briefly, under the Prime Minister Ramsay MacDonald. The ferment was at its worst in 1926 when the General Strike took place – miners, transport workers and millions of others stopped work for ten days. There were no trains or buses running and no newspapers. The newly formed BBC proved its value, as radio was the only way people could learn what was going on. Again the King urged moderate behaviour on his Prime Minister (the Conservative, Stanley Baldwin) who might have adopted harsh measures against the strikers.

Times were even harder from 1929 to 1931. During these years (known as 'the slump') there was world-wide economic trouble, businesses closed down, and millions were out of work. In order to help, the King stepped in and persuaded all three political parties to pull together in one government – a coalition.

Meantime many countries in the British Empire began to demand independence, as they were tired of being ruled from London. In 1931 the Empire was changed into a Commonwealth comprising self-governing dominions (for example, Australia and Canada), with some smaller colonies in Africa, etc. still controlled from London. India was to be only semi-independent (until 1947). The King continued to be head of the Commonwealth.

To the end of his days, the favourite recreations of George the 'sailor king' were racing his yacht *Britannia*, and stamp-collecting (his famous collection can be seen in the British Museum). He had none of his father's fondness for parties and frivolity. His serious-mindedness and common sense during such troubled times made him not only a good king but a popular one too, and the whole nation grieved when he died.

Edward VIII 1936

Age 42. Son of George V. Married Mrs Wallis Simpson (American).
No children. Abdicated.

The new king reigned for only a few months. His intention to marry
Mrs Simpson, who had divorced two husbands, created a major crisis –
for England's monarchs are bound by their adherence to the Church's
teaching never to marry a divorced person. The Government and the
Archbishop of Canterbury urged him to break with Mrs Simpson. This
he refused to do, choosing abdication and exile rather than lose the
woman he loved.

George VI 1936–1952

Age 41–57. Son of George V. Married Elizabeth Bowes-Lyon (Scottish).
Two children. Buried at Windsor.

As a result of Edward VIII's abdication, his younger brother George came
unexpectedly to the throne. He was a shy man with a stammer, who
would have much preferred a quiet family life to wearing the crown.
And the monarchy was now rather unpopular after all the scandal and
gossip that had surrounded Edward and Mrs Simpson. George was,
however, far more conscientious than his elder brother. Not very
successful in the naval career that had been chosen for him, he had,
however, shown real understanding when he became involved in
studying industrial affairs and in running camps for working-class boys.

Like his father, he was soon faced with the horrors of a world war
started by Germany, and once again both King and Queen shared their
people's dangers and hardships during the bombing raids on Britain, so
that, when Hitler was at last defeated, they had both become greatly
loved and admired. George had seen the terrible effects the 1914–18 war
had had on Britain, but he realized the need to support other European
countries against the spread of Nazism. Just before the war began, he had
visited America to strengthen Britain's ties there, for he realized that in
any war American support could be vital. During the war, he travelled

to war zones in North Africa and Malta, and went to Normandy just after the D-Day landings that led to final victory.

This war had been fought not only to curb the spread of Hitler's dictatorship throughout Europe, but also to stop the evil spread of anti-semitism. In Germany millions of Jews were suffering or dying terrible deaths in concentration camps, and even in Britain there had been anti-Jewish demonstrations staged by Mosley and his Fascist followers.

When peace came, George VI saw Britain change dramatically, particularly in the years when the Labour Party was in power. One by one the Government took over, wholly or partly, the ownership and running of such vital industries as the coal-mines, railways, gas and electricity supplies, etc. Hospitals and doctors, too, were 'nationalized' and brought into the Government's Health Service. Family allowances were started and National Insurance was extended. The 'welfare state' had arrived, meaning that the Government saw its principal responsibility for the first time to be a concern for the people's welfare.

In science and industry too there were major developments. Many everyday things now taken for granted had their beginnings in George's reign: television, paperbacks, nylon stockings, ballpoint pens, detergents, tape-recorders and transistors, plastics like polythene and fabrics like Terylene, computers, DDT, supersonic planes, long-playing records and 'wonder drugs' like penicillin and cortisone.

After the war literature and art took a completely new turn too. New names became famous – among the writers, Evelyn Waugh, George Orwell, W. H. Auden, Graham Greene, Dylan Thomas, T. S. Eliot, Stephen Spender and James Joyce; in the arts, Graham Sutherland and Henry Moore; and in the cinema and theatre, Laurence Olivier, Vivien Leigh and Noël Coward.

During these years of change and of stress, George was fortunate to have such a sensible and helpful wife as Elizabeth, a Scottish commoner who turned into an ideal twentieth-century queen, still immensely popular today as Queen Mother. Her charm and friendliness more than made up for the fact that George himself seemed to some people a bit aloof and formal. Yet despite the formality, most were aware how much he loved his country and how very hard he worked for his people until, after several illnesses, the tired King died in his sleep one night.

Elizabeth II 1952—

Age 26–. Daughter of George VI. Married Philip (Greek-born, British-naturalized). Four children.

Elizabeth had grown up during World War II, and as soon as she was old enough she persuaded her parents to let her do National Service, just like every other girl at her age in 1945. Second Lieutenant Elizabeth Windsor became a skilled driver and motor-mechanic but, more important, she lived and worked with the ordinary people who were her father's subjects, and learnt about their hopes and their problems. Two years later she married Philip, a prince of the Greek royal family who had become a naturalized British citizen and was later created Duke of Edinburgh.

Together they have helped to create much goodwill for Britain at a period when the country's power and reputation abroad have declined. No monarch has travelled as much as Elizabeth II, visiting not only Commonwealth countries but Europe and America too – sometimes carrying out exhausting tours in places where there have been dangerous demonstrations against Britain. Everywhere huge crowds applaud her with an enthusiasm that no political leader has ever inspired.

In the first twenty years of her reign, Britain changed from a country still suffering from the war, particularly where the shortage of houses was concerned, to 'an affluent society' in which the majority of people had high wages to spend on cars, TVs, etc., and little fear of unemployment. Now the situation is changing somewhat, as not even bigger wages keep up with rising prices, and there is hardship among old people on low pensions. Taxation too has been heavy in order to pay for things like huge defence costs at times when a war with Russia seemed possible; and for more welfare, like extending free education up to the age of sixteen. Even so, there has been a transformation in the living style of millions for whom things like central heating, colour television, nylon carpets, record players, drip-dry clothes, supermarkets, package holidays abroad, launderettes, pop music, bingo and betting shops have made life easier or more colourful.

Whether life is also better is another matter. Violence is a growing problem, with racial hostilities where immigrants live, religious troubles in Ireland, and more violent crimes. Strikes affect thousands of workers; and there are more divorces, unmarried mothers, and children who do not have a good home-life with their parents.

Queen Elizabeth, unlike many monarchs in the past, is the head of a united and happy family, conscientiously carrying out the duties the nation expects of her. In a world of rapidly shifting values, the monarchy is now a steadying influence. That is why the loyalty and affection inspired by Elizabeth II are at least as great as those given to any previous king or queen in British history.

Royal places to visit

The following are just some of the places still to be seen which bring alive the history of the kings and queens of England. You will find more as you travel about. In places like the National Portrait Gallery, stately homes and museums (and on many inn signs) their portraits are to be seen; and their statues stand in the streets and in many cathedrals. Their battle-grounds are now turned into busy roads or quiet fields and just the names survive, with perhaps a small memorial tablet to mark the spot.

Henry VIII left his mark in the many ruins of monasteries to be seen (as did the Roundheads when they wrecked church windows and statues). But the memorials of other monarchs are the schools, colleges, libraries and cathedrals which they brought into being, some bearing their names to this day, and their palaces or castles now open to the public.

Berkshire
Eton   Eton College was founded by Henry VI.
Reading   The abbey contains the grave of Henry I.
Windsor   Windsor Castle has been the home of many monarchs and contains many of their tombs (Victoria is buried in Frogmore Mausoleum nearby). In the castle is Edward III's chapel for the Knights of the Garter.

Buckinghamshire
Penn   The church here contains the memorial Victoria erected to her beloved Disraeli.

Cambridgeshire
Cambridge   Some of the university colleges were founded by Henry III, VI and VIII. Edward VII and George VI were students at Trinity College.
Peterborough   In the cathedral are the original graves of Mary Queen of Scots and Catherine of Aragon, wife of Henry VIII.

Cheshire
Chester   From Phoenix Tower Charles I watched his army being defeated nearby.

Cumbria
Barrow-in-Furness   The abbey was founded by King Stephen.
Burgh-by-Sands   A memorial marks where Edward I died on his way to fight Robert Bruce.

Carlisle   The castle was built by William II – Mary Queen of Scots was imprisoned here.

Kendal   Kendal Castle was the birthplace of Catherine Parr, wife of Henry VIII. She lived at the nearby Sizergh Castle after his death.

Penrith   Richard III stayed at the house that is now the Gloucester Arms.

Derbyshire

Chesterfield   Revolution House was the meeting-place of plotters to bring William and Mary to the throne.

Devonshire

Brixham   The landing-place of William III.

Newton Abbot   William III was proclaimed king at St Leonard's Tower.

Plymouth   The museum has a gold cup that Elizabeth I gave to Drake after he had sailed round the world.

Dorset

Corfe Castle   King John lived in the castle, Edward II was imprisoned here, and it was blown up in the Civil War.

Sherborne   Charles II hid at Trent Manor while on the run.

Weymouth   George III often stayed at what is now the Gloucester Hotel.

East Sussex

Battle   The abbey and museum here commemorate the battle of Hastings.

Brighton   The Pavilion was created for George IV. The tomb of his wife Mrs Fitzherbert is in St John's Catholic Church (she lived at 55 The Steine).

Lewes   The town walls were built by Henry III. In a battle nearby he was defeated by Simon de Montfort.

Pevensey   William the Conqueror landed here.

Essex

Waltham Cross   In the High Street stands one of Edward I's Eleanor crosses.

Gloucestershire

Berkeley   Edward II was murdered in the castle.

Cheltenham   George III 'took the waters' at the spa baths.

Gloucester   The cathedral contains the tomb of Edward II, and Henry III was crowned here. Lady Jane Grey was proclaimed queen at the New Inn.

Moreton-in-Marsh   Charles I stayed at the White Hart.

Hampshire

Milford-on-Sea   Charles I was imprisoned at the nearby Hurst Castle.

Netley   The abbey was founded by Henry III.

New Forest   Not far from Minstead is a stone which marks where William II was killed.

Porchester   The castle was built by Henry II; Henry V assembled his army here before Agincourt.

Portsmouth   The docks were founded by Henry VIII. Charles II was married at Government House.

Southsea   The castle was built by Henry VIII.

Titchfield   Charles I was arrested at the abbey.

Winchester   William II is buried in the cathedral.

Hereford and Worcester

Hereford   The cathedral contains King Stephen's chair.

Worcester   The cathedral contains King John's tomb.

Hertfordshire

Berkhamsted   The castle was built by William I.

Hatfield   Mary I and Elizabeth lived at the Old Palace when they were princesses.

Isle of Wight

Cowes   Queen Victoria spent childhood holidays at Norris Castle; she later lived (and died) at Osborne House, near Cowes.

Newport   Charles I was imprisoned at Carisbrooke Castle and at the Grammar School.

Jersey

St Helier   Charles II took refuge at Elizabeth Castle.

Kent

Canterbury   In the cathedral Henry II did penance for the murder of Thomas Becket; it also contains the tombs of Henry IV and the Black Prince (son of Edward III).

Dover   Richard I assembled his crusaders at the castle.

Hever   Henry VIII met Anne Boleyn at the castle, which he later gave to Anne of Cleves.

Leeds   The castle was the home of many queens.

Margate   William III often stayed at Quex House.

Ramsgate   Elizabeth I occupied the Old House.

Rochester   Charles II stayed at Restoration House on his return to the throne; James II stayed at another house here before his exile. The castle was besieged by John.

Sevenoaks   Nearby is Knole, a large estate, the house of which contains a bedroom that was sumptuously furnished for James I.

Lancashire

Preston   James I stayed at Hoghton Tower and knighted a joint of beef 'Sir Loin'.

Leicestershire

Leicester   Richard III's body was brought to a house here after the battle of Bosworth.

Market Harborough   Charles I stayed in a house here before the battle of Naseby.

Lincolnshire

Grantham   King John held a court at the Angel Hotel. Richard III signed the death warrant of the rebel Duke of Buckingham here.

Lincoln   The castle was built by William I and later captured by King Stephen from Matilda. Henry II was crowned in Lincoln Cathedral as well as in London. Edward I and II held parliaments in the cathedral which also holds a copy of Magna Carta.

The Wash   King John lost the crown jewels here.

London

Albert Memorial   Erected by Queen Victoria in memory of her husband.

Banqueting House   Charles I was executed outside.

British Museum   Contains a copy of Magna Carta and various royal exhibits, including George V's stamp collection.

Buckingham Palace   The home of monarchs from George III onwards. The Gallery exhibits paintings they collected and their state coaches can be seen in the Mews.

Greenwich   The Queen's House was built for Anne, wife of James I.

Houses of Parliament   Houses the throne used by monarchs when opening Parliament. Under the building is the cellar where the gunpowder plot against James I was discovered.

Kensington Palace   Victoria lived here as a child.

National Gallery   This gallery was started by George IV.

Regent's Park and Regent Street   Designed for George IV when Prince Regent.

Royal Academy   Founded by George III.

St James's Palace   This was built by Henry VIII.

Science Museum   Contains the scientific instruments of George III.

Tower of London   This was the fortress-palace of many monarchs (and sometimes their prison or murder site). Lady Jane Grey was executed here. The crown jewels are kept here and you can also see the Yeomen of the Guard or 'beefeaters' corps originally founded by Henry VII.

Westminster Abbey   Houses the tombs of many monarchs, the coronation throne, and effigies of monarchs.

Westminster Hall   This was built by Richard II. The trial of Charles I was held here.

Norfolk

Castle Rising · Isabella, widow of Edward II, was imprisoned in the castle.

Sandringham   Elizabeth II's country home. George VI was born and died there and the church has memorials to Edward VII.

Northamptonshire

Geddington and Northampton   Both have Eleanor crosses erected by Edward I.

Naseby   Charles I was defeated in battle here and imprisoned later at Holdenby House.

Northumberland

Bamburgh   Edward IV besieged Margaret (Henry VI's wife) in the castle.

Berwick-upon-Tweed   The castle and city walls were built by Edward I as defences against the Scots. In the parish church he heard Bruce's claim to the Scottish throne. Wark Castle nearby played a part in Edward II's Scottish wars.

North Yorkshire

Knaresborough   Richard II was imprisoned in John of Gaunt's castle.

Pickering   Richard II was kept in Pickering Castle after he abdicated.

Scarborough   Richard III stayed in a house here.

York   Edward II's Parliament met in York Minster; their shields are painted on stone around the nave. Edward III was married here.

Nottinghamshire

East Stoke   Here Henry VII captured Lambert Simnel the imposter.

Harby   There is a memorial in the church to Eleanor, wife of Edward I, who died here.

Newark   King John died in the castle.

Nottingham   Edward III arrested Mortimer in the castle.

Southwell   Charles I surrendered at the Saracen's Head and was then imprisoned at Hampton Court (Surrey).

Oxfordshire

Oxford   Some of the university colleges were founded by Henry III, Edward II and others. Edward VII was a student at Christ Church for a year (living at Frewen Hall), in the great hall of which Elizabeth I watched a play. Richard I was born at the castle, which played a part in King Stephen's war with Matilda.

Scotland

Balmoral Castle   The family holiday home of the royal family for over a century.

Bannockburn   Robert Bruce won Scotland's independence in the famous battle there.

Culloden Moor   Bonnie Prince Charlie was defeated at the battle of Culloden in 1746.

Falkland Palace   A favourite house of Mary Queen of Scots.

Glamis Castle   Childhood home of Queen Elizabeth the Queen Mother.

Linlithgow Palace   Mary Queen of Scots was born there.

Loch Leven Castle   Mary Queen of Scots was imprisoned there in 1567 but escaped.

The Palace of Holyroodhouse   Official Scottish residence of the Queen.

Stirling Castle   Mary Queen of Scots and James VI lived there.

Shropshire

Ludlow   Edward V and his brother lived in the castle before their murder in the Tower of London.

Shrewsbury   Charles I and James I stayed at the Council House. The museum has the cloak Charles I wore at his execution. Henry VII lodged at a house in the town on his way to the battle of Bosworth. Mary I lived at the Old House for a while. Shrewsbury School was one of many founded by Edward VI. Battlefield Church nearby commemorates the battle of Shrewsbury at which Henry IV defeated rebels.

Tong   In nearby Boscobel House grounds stands the successor to the oak in which Charles II hid all day.

Somerset
Glastonbury   Edward I had the supposed bones of King Arthur reburied in front of the altar in the abbey.
Sedgemoor   Monmouth's rebels were defeated by James II.
Taunton   Henry VII tried Perkin Warbeck the impostor at the castle, Royalists besieged it in the Civil War and Monmouth's rebels were executed there.

Staffordshire
Mosely Old Hall   Charles II took refuge here after the battle of Worcester.
Stafford   Charles I stayed at High House.

Suffolk
Framlingham   Mary I stayed in the castle during Lady Jane Grey's attempt on the throne.
Newmarket   The racecourse here was started by James I. In the town are the remains of a palace of Charles II, and the house of Nell Gwynn.

Surrey
Dorking   George VI spent his honeymoon at a house called Polesden Lacey near here.
Hampton Court   This was the palace given to Henry VIII by Wolsey. Charles I was imprisoned here.
Kew   The Royal Botanic Gardens were founded by George III and Kew Palace was one of his homes. The Public Records Office here keeps the Domesday Book and a copy of Magna Carta.
Richmond   The Palace was built by Henry VII. Elizabeth I died there. White House in Richmond Park was the birth-place of Edward VIII.
Runnymede   In these meadows near Egham, King John sealed Magna Carta.

Wales
Caernarvon, Conway, Harlech, Beaumaris and Caerphilly   Each of these places has a castle built by Edward I.
Monmouth   Henry V was born at Monmouth Castle.

Warwickshire
Compton Wynyates   Henry VIII slept in a room here.
Edge Hill   Charles I's first battle in the Civil War was fought here.

Kenilworth   The castle was besieged by Henry III, enlarged by John of Gaunt, visited by Henry VIII, and given by Elizabeth I to Robert Dudley who often feasted her there.

West Midlands

Birmingham   Charles I stayed at Aston Hall.

Coventry   Henry VII stayed at St Mary's Hall – a huge tapestry illustrates this – and Mary Queen of Scots was imprisoned here.

West Sussex

Arundel   The castle was besieged by Henry I and King Stephen.

Horsham   The Bluecoat School was founded by Edward VI – the boys still wear the costume of his time.

Shoreham-by-Sea   In St Nicholas Church is the grave of the ship's captain who took Charles II to France.

West Yorkshire

Pontefract   Richard II was murdered in Pontefract Castle.

Wiltshire

Burbage   At Wolf Hall Jane Seymour and Henry VIII met.

Salisbury   At the King's Arms, Royalists organized Charles II's escape after the battle of Worcester.

Woodford   Heale House was one of Charles II's hiding-places.

Also by Elizabeth Gundrey in Piccolo

Sewing Things 35p

Everything you need to know about sewing, from choosing the patterns, colours and materials to decorating the finished articles.

Growing Things 25p

Have fun growing things even if you haven't got a garden!

Collecting Things 30p

Exciting and practical ideas on how to start over 100 collections.

Joining Things 45p

Lots of ideas for joining clubs.

Make Your Own Monster 25p

How to make models and pictures of monsters, dress up as monsters, act plays with monsters ...

Making Decorations 25p

Fun in the Garden 50p

William Vivian Butler
The Greatest Magicians on Earth 40p

A history of magicians from Merlin up to the present day, with accounts of their feats, tricks, illusions, miracles and spells.

Margery Morris
Stories of the Ancient Britons 50p

From the old Stone Age to the Roman invasion, here are fascinating stories of the hunters, miners, archers, priests, warriors and their children, who lived in Ancient Britain.

Lloyd and Jennifer Laing
The Young Archaeologist's Handbook 40p

Archaeology? Why not have a go?
This is an unusual book which shows you how to make a 'find' and document it, how to plan an expedition, how to use the museums, and what to look out for in town and in the countryside.

You can buy these and other Piccolo books from booksellers and newsagents; or direct from the following address:
Pan Books, Cavaye Place, London SW10 9PG
Send purchase price plus 20p for the first book and 10p for each additional book, to allow for postage and packing

While every effort is made to keep prices low, it is sometimes necessary to increase prices at short notice. Pan Books reserve the right to show on covers new retail prices which man differ from those advertised in the text or elsewhere